Consider It
PURE
Joy

Cynthia,
Trust God!
Trust the process!

Gift from Vicky Washington
Sunday Aug. 5, 2018
also Ride home ? Fai Nelson came
to take me to Church
also Thank You —
Lord for your many
Blessing !!!.
♡ ♡ ♡
Lord

JENNIFER JONES AUSTIN

Consider It Pure Joy
by Jennifer Jones Austin

© 2018 by Jennifer Jones Austin

Published by The Church Online, LLC

For information, address the publisher:

The Church Online, LLC
1000 Ardmore Blvd.
Pittsburgh, PA 15221

International Standard Book Number: 978-1-940786-61-2

Library of Congress Catalogue Card Number: Available Upon Request

Printed in the United States of America

First Edition: February 2018

Endorsements

"Jennifer Jones Austin writes like an angel who has been "to hell and back" with her faith in God paying for the round-trip ticket. *Consider It Pure Joy* makes you want to give Ms. Jones Austin a standing ovation for her inspirational courage in the face of a life-threatening disease. Her remarkable attitude of gratitude for the process she endured shows us how to transform grief into a gift. This uplifting and compelling page turner will be my go-to ministry resource that I will recommend to all whose lives are turned upside down because of a dire diagnosis."

Frederick Douglass Haynes, III, Senior Pastor, Friendship West Baptist Church, Dallas, Texas

"With grounded humor, transparency, and discipline, *Consider It Pure Joy* walks us through an incredible journey of courage and faith. From the moment Jennifer Jones Austin understood her diagnosis as something "bigger than me," through her determination to be "here until I'm not here," and the acceptance of her promotion to a deeper vocation to tell a new story of God's boundless grace, the reader becomes witness to a soulful meditation on transformational joy. I found myself crying, laughing, squirming, praying, stopping to marvel at God's power, grateful for the Spirit of revival, breathing sighs of relief, and finally, determined to live on purpose, too."

Dr. Emma Jordan-Simpson, Executive Pastor, Concord Baptist Church of Christ, Brooklyn, New York

"Jennifer Jones Austin has given the world a gift with this beautiful, breathtakingly visceral account of what she describes as a gift: her epic battle with cancer. Her vivid descriptions of the journey, threaded together with raw honesty and courageous vulnerability, will challenge you to stay awake to all that God dreams for your life . . . and to intentionally live your life's purpose with joy."

Rev. Dr. Amy K. Butler, Senior Minister, The Riverside Church, New York, New York

"What a journey of pure faith! Jennifer Jones Austin's journey with cancer, as artfully told in *Consider It Pure Joy*, is far beyond anything the purveyors of prosperity gospel, the guardians of staid Protestantism, or the fathers of formulaic Catholicism could ever fathom. Hers is a mystic's walk through the valley of the shadow of death. It's the experience of the desert fathers and mothers, where little stood between them and the demons that tried to destroy them but God, and God alone. It is an utterly unique experience."

Rev. Frederick A. Davie, Executive Vice President, Union Theological Seminary

"Jennifer Jones Austin's narrative is a personal testimony to the triumph of faith in the face of life-threatening adversity. You feel the excruciating pain of her experience along with her, while marveling at her ability to consider the journey a true blessing. Completely captivating, *Consider It Pure Joy* is a gift to anyone who needs inspiration to overcome challenges that seem impossible."

David Banks, CEO and President, The Eagle Academy Foundation

"'A part of me was being sucked out of me, and that part was going to tell me my future.' These are the words of Jennifer Jones Austin, one of my heroes in the faith, as she faced a bone marrow biopsy. The prognosis? Cancer! But she knew her future would not be determined by prognosis, but by the faith she knew from a child. *Consider It Pure Joy* tells her story—with boldness, transparency, and vulnerability. Some stories stay with you for life. This is one of them!"

Rev. A.R. Bernard, founder and CEO of the Christian Cultural Center, Brooklyn, New York

"*Consider It Pure Joy* is a must-read for everyone facing a seemingly insurmountable test. This true and compelling story shows how a person can survive the highs and lows of their greatest challenge, learning to trust the process with faith, courage, and pure joy. This is a story of tenderness, transparency, tenacity, and triumph!"

Dr. Claybon Lea, Jr., Pastor, Mount Calvary Baptist Church, Fairfield and Suisun City, California

"The first time I read *Consider It Pure Joy*, I found myself swept up in an enormously compelling story. I went back and read it again, stopping deliberately along the way to absorb its many rich and rewarding spiritual insights more fully. I have now read the entire book through a third time. It is still offering new gems of reflection. Jennifer Jones Austin has given us an extraordinary gift. She takes us with her to the very edge of life not once, but several times in these pages. Each time she opens a new window onto the beauty of life and the power of faith. *Consider It Pure Joy* is far more than one woman's story of surviving cancer. It is about finding the meaning of life and the purpose of our existence on this earth."

Dale T. Irvin, President and Professor of World Christianity, New York Theological Seminary

"In her debut book, *Consider It Pure Joy*, Jennifer Jones Austin details her epic battle with leukemia and the power of faith and action. Her story of how she, a brilliant activist with an unmatched passion to combat poverty and injustices in our nation, overcame devastating odds by turning to community to help cure her of a deadly disease is a testament of resilience that will help others find strength in adversity."

Rev. Al Sharpton, President of National Action Network

"Read this book. Walk down every page of gripping emotion. *Consider It Pure Joy* enables a partnership with those whose life script includes a reset from trauma, but its true value is as a much-needed reminder that while doctors treat and families keep the faith, only God cures. And such mercy begs us to know the reason for our lives."

Dr. Rudolph Franklin Crew, President, Medgar Evers College, New York

"In this powerful personal story, Jennifer Jones Austin teaches us that real joy is not mere happiness determined by our situations, but rather it's a deeper emotion informed by faith, hope, and courage that enables us even in the midst of shedding tears and experiencing fears to keep on keeping on. *Consider It Pure Joy* challenges and inspires. This book is a must-read!"

Bishop William J. Barber II, Founder and National President/ Senior Lecturer of Repairers of the Breach

Dedication

To all who thought I was worth saving, especially
the 13,000+ who didn't even know me.

TABLE OF CONTENTS

Introduction...17

Chapter One: Diagnosis.....................................19

Chapter Two: Prognosis.....................................31

Chapter Three: The Real Prognosis.....................43

Chapter Four: Submission...................................47

Chapter Five: Embracing My Reality....................53

Chapter Six: Heading Home................................65

Chapter Seven: The Cancer Club.........................73

Chapter Eight: Purpose......................................79

Chapter Nine: Holding Two Truths......................85

Chapter Ten: Chosen...95

Chapter Eleven: Putting My Story Out There.......105

Chapter Twelve: Should I Die.............................111

Chapter Thirteen: #SaveJenAustin.....................121

Chapter Fourteen: Just One Match......................125

Chapter Fifteen: Always....................................133

Chapter Sixteen: Send Me a Sign.......................143

Chapter Seventeen: Preparing for Transplant.......155

Chapter Eighteen: Transplant............................165

Chapter Nineteen: Post-Transplant.....................179

Chapter Twenty: It Ain't Over 'til It's Over...........189

Afterword: Awake in the Moment.......................193

Acknowledgements...217

Biography...219

Introduction

Ever since becoming ill, friends, family, colleagues, and even strangers with whom I shared my cancer experience have encouraged me to write a book about my ordeal. For several years I dismissed the suggestion, believing there was no need for another survivor story. When I was sick, especially in those first days following my initial induction into the world of cancer and chemotherapy, books about various cancer experiences were coming at me from every which way. They all were helpful and provided me with the information and the hope I needed to help me deal. I never longed or wished for a book that would address some unanswered question.

But then one day it occurred to me that there is room. There is need for at least one more book. Of all the more than fifty books I received about the ups and downs of cancer—the "what to expect" type books, and the "how to" books—never had I encountered one that illuminates the gift that can be yours in battling cancer, serious illness, or some other major life challenge. Yes, the gift of fighting for your life, and being awake in the moment to appreciate the journey.

This book is about the amazing journey that can be had when fighting a life-threatening disease or some other life-altering test, no matter what the outcome. I thought I should write my story, and in doing so, share the gift.

CHAPTER
ONE

Diagnosis

Finally, I get to sit back and rest. It's 8:30 PM on a hot night in late August. Worn down after more than twelve hours of meetings, emails, and phone calls, I'm in a taxi cab and I'm heading to Brooklyn. I'm going home. I'm tired, but I'm still looking at emails on my BlackBerry when the TV in the taxi catches my attention. The story of a child who desperately needs a bone marrow transplant is playing on the loop. Information is being broadcast about donor drives that will be held in New York City over the coming weekend to find her a bone marrow donor and cure her of cancer.

I think, *I'd love to help. I want to help. How can I fit the drive in this weekend?* And then, I remind myself of all I must do. Rolling out the United Way of New York City's Community Impact Plan at work. The kids going back to school. *I can't do this right now,* I think. *I can't take time off right now and be hospitalized for several days to give marrow. My kids need me. I have to move this work plan forward. I want to, but I can't right now. There will be lots of people who come out for her. She'll get a match. She'll be okay.*

September 2009 seemed no different than other Septembers in recent years. Summer vacation was over, the kids were back in school, my husband, Shawn, and I were back at work, and "birthday mania" was upon us. Shawn's birthday was just a few days away on the 21st, our daughter Kennedy's on the 23rd, my mom's on the 28th, Shawn's brother Matt's on the 30th, and mine on October 1. September would be no different than it had been since Kennedy was born twelve years earlier—chock full of back-to-school activities and birthday celebrations.

Then again, it would be different, and excitingly so. Mom was turning seventy, and we were having a surprise birthday party for her at our home in Brooklyn Saturday evening, September 19. All of her children and grandchildren—Billy and his children, Bill, Justice, and Brooklyn; Elsa and her children, Natalia and Brian; Lesley and her husband, Randy; and Shawn and me and ours, Kennedy and Channing—would be here.

Mom knew that we all would be in town for the weekend, but it hadn't dawned on her that she was the main reason why. As far as she was concerned, all four of her children, two sons-in-law, and seven grandchildren would be in town to witness the co-naming of MacDonough Street in Bedford Stuyvesant, Brooklyn to "Rev. Dr. William Augustus Jones Way."

For months, I had been working with Reverend Peyton—at the time the interim pastor of Bethany Baptist Church in Bedford Stuyvesant—and other community leaders and elected officials to secure approval to co-name MacDonough Street after my daddy. For forty-three years, my father had pastored Bethany Baptist Church, which ran the entire block of Marcus Garvey Boulevard between MacDonough and Decatur Streets. To say he was a pillar of the community right up until he passed away in 2006 would be an oversimplification. In addition to pastoring one of the largest churches in all of New York City, he was both a local and national civil rights and social justice leader whose vast efforts helped bring an end to discrimination and social and economic injustice by various institutions including major corporations, hospitals and health systems, the media, and government. During the summer, the community board voted in favor of co-naming the street, and the ceremony was set for the third Saturday in September, in keeping with the tradition of celebrating Dad's pastoral anniversary at Bethany. Having led the co-naming effort for the family, I was invited to speak at the event.

Like I always do, to the relief of some and the displeasure of others, I planned the weekend pretty much to the minute, and tried to ensure all major details were taken care of. We all would go to the ceremony Saturday morning, then Lesley and Randy would keep Mom entertained in the afternoon while the rest of us handled last-minute, day-of-party preparations. Later that evening, after Mom's friends had arrived at our home, Lesley and Randy would bring her there. She would never catch on.

As the weekend drew closer, I spent my evening hours juggling the final catering details for the party, writing my remarks for the street co-naming ceremony, responding to work emails, tending to my children and their back-to-school needs, and outlining my committee's responsibilities and timeline as co-chair of my Jack and Jill chapter's biannual fundraiser. Needless to say, I was tired—very tired.

On the Wednesday evening before the big weekend, I attended Kennedy's middle school's open school night to meet her new teachers and learn about the curriculum and instruction planned for the semester. As I walked from one class to another, I passed another mom, Jamie, in the hallway. She asked me how I was, and I casually responded, "Tired." Indeed I was.

I got home later that night at about 9:30 PM and jumped on a Jack and Jill fundraiser call. Our chapter of the African American mothers' organization was raising money to fund college scholarships for high school seniors in the Brooklyn community. Three hours later at about 12:40 AM, my co-chair, Pamela, and I were finally hanging up. Others had gotten off the call a while before. I had been sharing with Pamela my weekend plans and how I felt both excited and tired. She replied that all would be wonderful but that I should get some rest. We said goodnight and I went to bed.

That next day, I woke up feeling a little under the weather. I checked my schedule on my BlackBerry calendar and decided to work from home in the morning and then head into Manhattan just to have lunch with Linda, my former boss, and another friend and co-worker, Raysa. I was eager to share with Linda the exciting work we had underway at United Way and to get her advice.

We met at a Vietnamese restaurant in lower Manhattan. I ordered soup, but when it came, I had no interest in it. I felt like I was coming down with a cold or a virus. So, I didn't eat. Neither Raysa nor Linda seemed to notice I wasn't eating, but if they did, they probably thought my enthusiastic and incessant chatter was the cause. After lunch, I went back home to rest.

Diagnosis

Friday morning came, and I met it with a fever. When it was time to jump out of bed and get moving, I felt weak. I reached for my BlackBerry on my nightstand, grabbed it, and checked my calendar: breakfast with Fatima, my friend and colleague, and a United Way Board Committee meeting at noon.

I called Fatima and told her I wasn't feeling well and needed to reschedule. She understood, and asked that I make sure someone called her later in the day to let her know how I was doing. I agreed, all the while thinking that I would call or have Shawn call even though it wouldn't be necessary. What I was feeling wasn't that serious. It was just a bug.

I stayed under the covers for the next few hours. Around 10:00 AM, I managed to drag myself out of bed and into the shower, and then to dress and put on makeup. Not feeling good enough to catch the subway, I called Yvette, my assistant, and she sent a car service to pick me up for the board meeting.

Armed with Tylenol, I fought the fever.

I got in the car and began making my way from Brooklyn to Manhattan, to my office on Park Avenue. On the way, as we exited the Williamsburg Bridge and entered Manhattan, I asked the driver to pull over. I had to throw up.

When I arrived at the office, I still felt sick. Not wanting to spread my germs, I opted to participate in the board committee meeting by way of phone from my office just down the hall from the boardroom. I was tired, achy, hot, and nauseous. I wasn't much good but I pushed through.

Chapter One

When the meeting ended, I hung around the office a little longer to finish up a few things—just long enough to be playfully admonished by my boss for still being there. At about 3:30 PM, I went home and climbed into bed. I fell right to sleep.

Several hours later, I woke up and was drenched with my own sweat. The fever was high and my body was fighting it as best it could, but I was succumbing. I was weak. With only fifteen feet separating my bed from my bathroom, I was repeatedly on my knees, crawling back and forth and praying that I'd make it to both the toilet and wastebasket in time.

My mother was at the house with me, watching Channing and his friend while Shawn was at a wine tasting we'd committed to attending. She insisted that I go to the hospital. Believing it was a run of the mill virus or flu, I chose not to.

When Saturday, the big day, came, I was determined to enjoy the weekend and all the festivities I had planned. I willed myself out of bed and into the shower, over to the dressing room adjacent to my bedroom to get my clothes, and then back to the chair in my bedroom. I stared at my beautiful Brooks Brothers tailored gray suit with pink pinstripes, the complementing button-down shirt, and the gorgeous black pumps I'd placed on the floor by the clothes, wishing they would jump onto my body. When that didn't happen, I just sat there, trying to muster up the energy to get dressed, and trying to convince myself I was feeling better and could go to the co-naming ceremony. Twenty minutes later, having only gotten as far as bra and panties on, I admitted to myself that I was too weak, and that the only place I should be going was the hospital.

A short while later, my bedroom door opened and family members began passing through. Dressed for the co-naming ceremony, they all looked great. My sister, Lesley, in her pretty mauve suit, would present my remarks. Kennedy in her black wrap dress, looking more mature than her nearly twelve years. My Channing looking so handsome in his navy blue suit. And my nieces and nephews, all impeccably dressed. Each one stepped into my bedroom to say hi before leaving for the ceremony. They all looked and moved with distinction and honor. They were proud of their dad and granddad, and he certainly would have been proud of them. I couldn't go, but the family would be well-represented.

As soon as they left, Shawn went to the driveway and got the car to take me to the hospital. Mommy was still at the house and wanted to come with us, but we insisted her place was at the ceremony. I also needed her to go with the rest of the family to keep our plans for her celebration on track. She reluctantly agreed, and we drove her to the ceremony. We then headed to the hospital. I lay in the backseat of the car, feeling completely drained and depleted.

We sat in the emergency room and waited for me to be seen. I took turns sipping on water and stumbling to the bathroom to throw it up or catch myself before I soiled my clothes. Even though I knew the liquid wouldn't stop running through my body, I didn't want to become any more dehydrated than I already was.

Finally, better than four hours after I arrived at the hospital, the doctor saw me. Without much fanfare, he examined me and determined that I probably had some bad virus. He advised me to go home, take a couple of Advil pills, and sleep it off. He never checked my blood counts.

I went home that evening to a house full of people. Mom's friends had arrived, and our family was there. The house was alive with people and music, and lots of good food and happiness. I climbed the stairs slowly with Shawn helping me take every step.

From my bedroom, I could hear the party. People were laughing and dancing. I longed to be downstairs with them having fun, but I was in no shape to do so. I was exhausted. I went to bed.

I woke up the next morning, Sunday, to the faces of my nieces and nephews. They were checking on me before going to church. I remember telling Natalia, one of my nieces, how good she looked. She had a new hairstyle with lots of soft curls that framed her beautiful face.

Off they went, along with Shawn, Channing, and Kennedy, and my siblings. I stayed at home with Mom. I still had a fever, and I was still throwing up and having diarrhea.

Night came again and then Monday morning. It was Shawn's birthday. Nothing had changed concerning my condition. I still was in bed with nausea and diarrhea. My brother and sisters were gone and their children too. Channing and Kennedy went to school, and Shawn went to work. Again, Mommy stayed home with me.

I slept throughout the day, pretty much waking up only when my clothes were wringing wet or when I had to crawl to the bathroom.

Though able to sleep, my rest wasn't peaceful—far from it! As I slept in the bed, weak and tired, I was visited by a spirit draped in black. Hovering over the bed, it spoke directly to me, saying it was a death angel. But instantly, another spirit dressed in white came and floated above me. Immediately I embraced it as the angel of life. I screamed and woke myself up. I knew then I was in trouble.

I guess I was more tired than frightened because I fell asleep again. And when I awoke the next time, I experienced a new reality. My vision was blurred. I could hardly see. I couldn't make anything out.

I screamed for Mom, and she came running up the stairs as fast as she could from the kitchen on the first floor to my bedroom on the second floor. I told her of the latest development. Together, we called my primary physician, who advised me to come in the next day.

That Tuesday morning, I could hardly move. Unable to stand and see, Shawn and Mom helped me dress. They got me in the car and off we went to Manhattan to see my doctor. When we arrived at the doctor's office, which was a new office location for me, I was too tired to stand and walk, and I couldn't make out objects clearly. I had to move slowly through the lobby. With my legs buckling at the knees, I held on to Mom and waited for the elevator. It couldn't come fast enough. When it did, it took forever to reach the floor on which my doctor's office was located.

The walk from the elevator to the office seemed a never-ending quest. Perhaps it was just one hallway, but it seemed to me to be a twisting maze with several turns and closed doors all along the way. By the time I made it to the office door, I was done. I couldn't even hold my head up. I signed in at the receptionist desk, feeling anxious about how long it would be before I'd be seen. However,

Chapter One

I was so visibly in distress that another woman who had been waiting her turn insisted I go before her when her name was called.

In the examination room, my doctor took one look at me and exclaimed, "You need to go to an emergency room by ambulance right away!" I was in crisis, and there was no readily apparent reason as to why. She called an ambulance for me, and told us that she had no control over where it would take us. It would be New York University Hospital or St. Vincent's.

Minutes later, I was rolled on a stretcher into the ER at St. Vincent's Hospital. Though not considered one of New York's best hospitals, it certainly wasn't the worst. Attending ER physicians immediately went to work on me. The Chief of Hematology and the Chief of Infectious Diseases were on high alert. They ran all kinds of tests, including tests for HIV and H1N1.

I remember the doctors asking me if I might have HIV. Certain I didn't but desperate for a lighthearted moment, I looked right at Shawn as I lay on the ER bed and jokingly exclaimed, "I don't think so. Do I?"

With an onslaught of doctors standing at my bedside—all asking questions, sometimes repeating themselves and each other—and with Shawn moving fervently in and out of the curtain-drawn, make-shift room, I knew that people were working at a desperate pace to figure out what was going on. By now it was abundantly clear that whatever I had was not just a run-of-the-mill virus.

What I didn't know but later found out was that Shawn was in constant communication with friends who could help expedite blood work test results because the doctors said it was imperative—life or death—that they had answers sooner rather than later.

Despite being given plenty of IV fluids, my fever hovered at 103.5 degrees. With no clear read on what was making me sick, the doctors admitted me to the hospital and moved me to another floor to manage my fever, run more tests, and observe me. More blood work and more tests, and within twenty-four hours of being admitted, the answers came. It was Wednesday, September 23, my daughter's twelfth birthday.

As I lay in the hospital bed with Shawn at my side, Dr. Halperin, the chief hematologist, entered the room. Standing at the foot of my bed, he began talking. I remember the moment so vividly. His voice was clear and his words were declarative. He said to me, "You have leukemia."

CHAPTER
TWO

Prognosis

I lay there in my hospital bed silently for a few seconds, just long enough for Dr. Halperin's words to penetrate. And once I'd fully absorbed them and their meaning—that I had cancer—I gently but firmly responded, "So what do we do?"

Dr. Halperin began speaking again. He said I had acute myeloid leukemia (AML), and that it was treatable with chemotherapy. He told us that many people do well with chemotherapy as the primary form of treatment. The cancerous cells are zapped and killed. Patients then move into remission, and often stay in remission for the remainder of their lives. These patients may be inconvenienced for a couple of months, but then they can resume normal lives replete with work, gym, play, etc.

Upon hearing his prognosis, I thought, *All right, chemo, recovery, and then back to work—all in a couple of months.* Certainly wasn't what I had planned for the fall, but it sounded doable. I'd be back to work at United Way and to the gym by November. Possibly. Okay, we'd make it work.

Shawn began making calls and sharing the news. He called my mother, my sisters, and my brother. He called my sister-friends, the name I use to refer to my girlfriends who are close like sisters.

He called my boss, my pastor, his parents, and our children's friends' parents.

Mom came directly from work to the hospital. She was wearing a beautiful, colorful skirt with geometric shapes in red, yellow, green, white, and black. She looked at me and her face instantly turned weary and sad. Seeing her sadness mixed with a hint of despair, I chased her eyes with mine. When I caught them, I locked on to them and declared, "It's just a part of my journey." I wanted to comfort her and let her know I was okay.

My sister, Elsa, rushed in from Connecticut. Seems like I was diagnosed, and instantly she appeared. It may have been the next day, but keeping track of time wasn't my focus anymore.

My sister-friends—Andrea, Anne, Ayo, and Kim—showed up at the hospital and surrounded my bed. They talked feverishly, perhaps out of nervousness, and a couple cried. I remember thinking that things would be okay, whatever the outcome. If I died, these women would help Shawn and my family raise my kids, and they would definitely make sure my kids knew who their mom was.

The next day, Dr. Halperin came again to my bedside. This time he was accompanied by a very young looking white man, a resident. Dr. Halperin informed me that I needed a bone marrow biopsy. The medical team knew I had leukemia but needed more information about the type of leukemia to decide upon the best treatment. An extracted piece of my bone and some marrow would give them that information.

A short while later that same day, the resident and a nurse returned to perform the biopsy. The resident looked young, very young. I remember worrying that he might not know what he was doing, but I didn't complain.

Standing on the left side of my bed, they began prepping me:

"Turn onto your left side and scrunch up your knees. That's right, like a baby in a fetal position. Okay, now take a deep breath. We're going to numb the area of your lower back surrounding your tailbone."

In went the needle.

Deep.

After a few minutes, "Okay, now you're going to feel a little pain as we draw out some marrow."

I felt it all right, both physically and emotionally. A part of me was being sucked out of me, and that part was going to tell me my future. It was a gnawing pain.

"Okay, now we're just going to get some of your bone."

And that's when the chiseling started.

I never saw what the doctor used, but I felt it. My bone was being chipped with what must have been a microscopic-sized hammer.

All of this to determine how deeply the cancer had penetrated my blood and bones.

Chapter Two

I don't remember much of what happened over the next few days. Just two brief moments of consciousness. I remember waking up from a deep sleep and seeing Jamie, the parent I had told I was tired on open school night just days before. She was sitting in the chair at the foot of my bed. I kept my eyes open just long enough to notice her sitting there calm and content, keeping me company even though I was no company for her. Jamie's presence brought me peace.

The other memory is of a scene that rattled me. I woke up to my pastor and other ministers praying over my body. Their praying was a welcomed sight. However, my pastor's disposition rocked me. That he was praying for me was not surprising, but when he finished praying he stepped back from my bed, and I saw his eyes. They were filled with tears. I knew then my situation was dire.

That was Friday, September 25, 2009, and that same day I began losing the ability to breathe on my own. After more tests, the doctors discovered the cancer was in my lungs. To help me breathe, they intubated me. They put a tube down my throat and pumped air in and out of my lungs.

Despite Dr. Halperin's earlier prognosis, now he was in serious doubt concerning my condition. It was much more complicated and grave than he'd initially thought. Upon further examination, he and the other doctors concluded that I had a 99 percent probability of death.

Dr. Halperin found Shawn and my sister, Lesley, in the waiting room, where they had been holed up along with several other family members and friends. Speaking in an exacerbated voice and at a level others could hear, though he probably didn't intend it, Dr. Halperin said to Shawn, "She's going fast. She probably won't make it through the weekend."

⌒

Despite his prognosis, Dr. Halperin consulted Dr. Roboz, a leading leukemia specialist at New York-Presbyterian Weill Cornell Medical Center, and together they decided to put me in a medically induced coma and blast me with chemotherapy. If there was any chance I might survive, it would be by taking such extreme measures. It was not just the best option—it was the only option.

Shawn continued calling family and friends, colleagues and acquaintances. Mom, Billy, Elsa, and Lesley did the same. They asked for prayers on my behalf, and people responded. The cry went out across the country: **"Jennifer Jones Austin, wife of Shawn, mother of Channing and Kennedy, daughter of Natalie and Dr. William Augustus Jones Jr., and sister of Billy, Elsa, and Lesley, needs your prayers. She's been stricken with leukemia and is in a coma. The doctors have said she's going to die. Jennifer needs our prayers."** So went the word.

And the prayers went up. Family members, friends, colleagues, my church family, congregations across the city and across the country, friends of the family, and friends of friends prayed for me. The doctors did too.

All while I slept.

⌒

October 3, 2009

"Hi Sweetheart! Happy Birthday!" Elsa exclaimed.

"It's not my birthday yet," I replied.

"Yes, it's October 3. You've been sleeping," Elsa continued. "Lesley and Billy were here to see you. They'll be back."

I replied, "You don't have to lie to me. It's okay."

Elsa drew closer to my face and whispered, "I'm not. They were here. Justice too. Look at all these cards people have sent you for your birthday. You've had so many calls and visitors. The waiting room has been flooded with people."

There had essentially been a takeover of the hospital waiting room, as I quickly learned. From the day I'd become comatose, family and friends occupied every chair and square foot of the waiting room. More than forty people at a time at all hours of the day and night, with several sleeping in chairs and covered in blankets bought at the nearby pharmacy and convenience store. Friends stocked the room with food and snacks so no one went hungry while keeping vigil.

Elsa was going on and on with pure joy and excitement in her voice. I guess, rightly so. I wasn't supposed to have survived the weekend, and it had been more than a week since the doctors had declared my death imminent. She held up two journals filled with letters written by those who had come to see about me—friends, children of friends, colleagues, cousins, bosses, and former bosses including Mayor Bloomberg. Every one of the letters offered words of hope and encouragement, as if dismissing the doctors' opinion that I was going to die.

I tried to take it all in. Somehow I did. I whispered to Elsa, "This is not about me."

With a puzzled face, she retorted, "Yes! They've come to see you."

I instantly but calmly replied, "No, this is bigger than me."

Shawn entered the room and explained to me what was happening. I was in the ICU. I'd come close to death, but I was holding on. I'd been asleep in a medically induced coma for ten days with a tube down my throat. I'd undergone multiple chemotherapy treatments to kill the cancer cells in my body. He said I needed a couple more treatments. I'd also had an endoscopy while comatose, and had managed to land a left hook on the gastroenterologist as she was performing the procedure. I guess the fight was stirring in me.

Shawn kissed my forehead. He said he'd been praying for me and that everyone we knew had been praying for me. He told me that people we didn't even know were praying. He said there were visitors outside of my room but they couldn't come in. Only family could see me, per doctor's orders.

I remember Kennedy and Channing weren't with Shawn, but I also don't remember thinking they should have been. Because I'd been told how grave my situation had been and still was, and because they were young, I probably didn't expect them.

Shawn did share that he brought the kids to the hospital to see me while I lay comatose. I later learned that the doctors, believing I would die, had suggested he bring them to see me one last time. And so he did. As I lay still in a bed of ice with a large tube down my throat and smaller tubes with wiry threads sewn into my neck and chest to carry chemo and other medications to my veins, my babies stood side by side, holding hands right outside my hospital room. They stared through a glass window at me, capturing what they had been forewarned might be their last look.

Mommy came into the room shortly after Shawn. She smiled at me the best she could, but that look of pain and worry I'd seen days before was still there. Her eyes were sad and her mouth was tightly closed, but her face still managed a slight smile. The kind of smile a mother manages when her little one has been injured but she doesn't want to let on to the child how bad the injury is and that she is scared.

Mom told me that while I was comatose and Billy was in New York, he had a couple of CDs with gospel songs made for me. She asked me if I wanted to hear them. I managed a faint, "Yes."

Using a portable CD player she had borrowed from Joyce, her friend since they were in kindergarten some sixty-five years earlier, Mom played one of the CDs Billy had made. I listened intently, clinging to every word in Hezekiah Walker's "Faithful is Our God," especially when he sang, "I'm reaping the harvest God promised me, take back what the devil stole from me."

Though out of the coma, my body was still tired. I was heavily sedated and my breathing wasn't good. Even though the tube had been taken out of my throat and I no longer needed breathing assistance, I was still having problems. My throat was irritated and sore, and I could hardly speak.

I couldn't even eat. Not that I wanted anything anyway. My appetite was gone, just like the strength that had left my body. But the doctors wouldn't even let me try. They were worried I would choke on my food. They told me I would need a swallowing specialist. I didn't even know there was such a profession.

I could hardly move my body. I hadn't moved for ten days. I'd been strapped down with belts. My hands and arms had been tied to the bed because I tried to pull the tubes out of my neck, chest, and arms.

My bottom was sore. It hurt a lot. I didn't know why, but one night while lying in the hospital bed I thought I figured it out. A male nurse came into my room when no one else was present. He started touching me—my bottom and my vagina. I thought, *What is he doing? Why is he bothering me? Why is he rolling me over on my side? This isn't right.* I wanted to scream, "Somebody help me!" But I didn't. I secretly longed for a female nurse, but he was taking care of me instead. *He is taking advantage of me,* I thought.

The male nurse was actually cleaning me up after I had soiled myself and the bed. But in my drug-filled and confused mind, he was a mean and ugly man, and I was helpless. I cringed when he appeared. I wonder now if he sensed my fear. I am curious as to why I never said anything. Perhaps deep down inside I knew I wasn't thinking clearly.

Within a few days of waking up from the coma, my breathing improved. Elsa was to thank for that. She watched the vitals monitor like a hawk watches its prey, and, like a hawk, she showed me no mercy. If my oxygen number was low, she admonished me to take shallow breaths, and she didn't let up. I quickly grew tired of hearing her mouth, and worked harder at breathing.

My mouth and throat were very dry. I asked for water and was told I couldn't have any. Because I'd been intubated, the medical staff was concerned that I may have forgotten how to swallow. So, I couldn't have any fluids. Not even ice chips. But I begged anyway for water or ice, or something that would quench my thirst.

Eventually, I wore the staff down and the team allowed me to have sponge pops. Shaped like lollipops and about half the size of Tootsie Roll Pops, the sponge pops held and released just enough liquid to coat my inner mouth, but not enough to choke on.

I sipped and sucked on the sponge pops, all the while thinking the whole thing was silly. Of course I could swallow. I'd been doing it all my life. But the reality was I couldn't. Though it had only been ten days that I was comatose and intubated, that period was indeed long enough for me to forget how to swallow and to have to be restrained from drinking and eating. Only after I demonstrated to the swallowing specialist that I was able to swallow liquids would soft foods such as pudding, Jell-O, and yogurt be permitted.

I started regaining a little bit of my strength every day, enough to sit up in bed and then in a special chair with a firm back, reading notes and cards from friends and family, and talking for a few seconds at a time on the phone. I didn't have much of a voice, but I tried anyway. I wanted to carry on conversations like I was well. I wanted to talk about things happening in other people's lives, not my own. I needed to feel like I wasn't as sick as I was, and I needed others to not see and treat me as sickly. I wanted them to see me just as they had always known me—as the friend and family member in control and handling my and others' business as best I could.

My bottom was still sore—unbearably sore. It took me fully waking up to realize that while comatose, I'd lain too long in my soiled bed in my own excrement. My skin on my buttocks was raw, blistery, and infected. I'd developed an excruciatingly painful ulcer. The pain was so agonizing that I couldn't lay flat, bottom-down, on the bed.

Still in the ICU, I received numerous drugs that took me in and out of lucidity. When I was able to think clearly, I was well aware of my situation and my surroundings. I knew who was in my room. I knew where Shawn was and what my mother was doing. I knew what treatments I was receiving, and the time of day. I knew who was in the waiting room sitting with my family.

When I was sedated, however, that was a whole other story. I had hallucinations of all types. There was the episode when I was certain my husband and my friend and colleague, Kathryn, had been kicked out of the hospital and banned from returning because they weren't satisfied with the hospital's care and were raising hell.

My sister-friend, Bernie, too. In my hallucinations, she, a real-life physician, was watching the doctors' every move, along with Joyce, my mother's childhood friend and a former hospital administrator. In my state of delirium, they too had been kicked out because they made the doctors anxious. I was creating all types of scenarios in my mind about people having my back and letting it be known. As people known to take a stand whenever times demand such, I knew they were fighting with me and for me. In my toxin-filled mind, they were just taking the fight to another level.

CHAPTER
THREE

The Real Prognosis

As I became more alert and aware of my surroundings and circumstances, I learned more about my condition. The chemotherapy appeared to have worked. The leukemia that had been in my lungs was no longer presenting. And even though that was a good thing and we all were grateful, the doctors warned us that my ordeal with leukemia was far from over. They told me that the biopsy revealed that I had a broken seventh chromosome, which indicated that the cancer was likely environmentally caused.

My mind began to wonder, *Environmental? What? Where? How? Was it 9/11 when I walked hand-in-hand with one child and pregnant with the other through the streets of what is now called Ground Zero, with soot and debris enveloping me as the World Trade Center Towers fell? Had I ingested something toxic that day? Was it the turpentine I swallowed as a toddler? What? When? How?*

I didn't ponder these questions too long. I couldn't. I'd never really know. I had learned long before that there are some questions to which I will never have answers. Besides, what did it matter? My treatment wasn't dependent on knowing, and it didn't help—physically or emotionally—to worry. I couldn't waste time wondering why or how. I didn't have time to dwell on a question for which the answer was pretty much impossible to prove. I was in the fight of my life, and I had to concentrate on that.

The prognosis wasn't good. My doctors were certain that the cancer would return, and that the only chance of my long-term survival would come in the form of a bone marrow transplant to replace my permanently damaged blood and marrow system.

The good news: I'd survived the first cancer attack.

The bad news: I would likely not survive another cancer attack without a transplant.

Reality set in. I had a different kind of leukemia, the kind that wouldn't let me alone after just a few treatments and a couple of months. I wasn't going to be like the patients Dr. Halperin told me about—the ones who are back to work and exercise in just a matter of weeks. Life was going to be very different than the life I had known, and not just for a little while—maybe forever different. It wasn't going to be easy.

One night as I lay in bed in the ICU, Shawn took my hand, and together we prayed. We asked God for complete healing. Not just for God to make me better, but rather to heal me completely. We didn't want for me to just remain in remission. We wanted the cancer gone. We wanted me to be well, completely well, like before I got sick. We knew God could fix it, that He could fix me.

Still, I was scared. I didn't want to die.

And so the Lord, knowing His child and my needs, spoke to me. While lying in my hospital bed, I had a dream.

The Real Prognosis

I was in an elevator, riding down to the ground floor. When the doors opened, I stepped out, fell right on my face, and skidded across a burning, hot lava floor. As I skidded, my mind could only think about how my skin was being shredded and burned.

When my body came to a screeching halt, I jumped up. I scanned my body with my eyes and hands. I touched my face. I wasn't burned. My skin wasn't in shreds. I was safe and unharmed.

I tried to catch my breath and to understand what happened, but I couldn't because the dream raced on to another horrific situation.

This time, I was on a bus that was barreling down the highway, speeding out of control. I was being hurled forward uncontrollably down the aisle of the bus, heading straight for the windshield. And then, just like it happened seconds before, my body came to a halting stop. I stopped just a few feet shy of the windshield.

And in that moment, I heard God speak to me. I heard Him clearly say, "Don't you know I will be with you always?" In that very instant I understood. Through my dream, God was letting me know, "This journey you're about to take—it's going to be rough, but I've got you and it's going to be okay."

I remained in the ICU for a few more days. Weeks later, I would learn that this particular ICU was considered "the door of no return." If you went in, the odds were that you weren't coming out—at least not alive.

In what seemed an eternity but in reality was just a few days, I learned to swallow and eat again, and I learned to sit upright in a chair. But it all felt surreal. How was it that just a few weeks before

Chapter Three

I'd been running, riding my bike, and lifting weights daily, and now I couldn't even sit in a chair without assistance?

CHAPTER
FOUR

Submission

Finally, the day that signified meaningful progress came. I was to be moved out of the ICU to a room and bed on the hematology and oncology floor of the hospital. Before I could go to my new room, however, I had to have a surgical procedure to place a port in my chest. My doctor had recommended it. He said it would prevent me from having to be pricked with needles round-the-clock as the medical and nursing staff drew my blood, gave me more chemotherapy, and fed me drugs intravenously to prevent infections.

Agreeing to the port came only after I embraced and accepted what it meant from a vanity point of view. For years, I'd done a pretty good job of keeping a flat stomach and a flawless complexion. A port in my chest would result in a scar. I guess my priorities had to shift.

A patient escort arrived at the ICU and began taking measures to ensure my safety during my transport to the operating room. He put on a yellow gown, mask, and gloves, and then draped my body with another yellow gown as I lay flat in the bed. It dawned on me that I was actually being transported in the bed I was lying in. But of course! I couldn't walk! It wasn't just that I had tubes stitched to my neck and arms; that alone would make walking difficult. I hadn't gotten out of the bed but once, and that was to try to sit and hold my torso up in a special chair. My muscles were in atrophy.

The escort and nurse gathered up my IV pole, the medicine drip machine and cords, and the vitals monitor. Whatever the escort couldn't carry was thrown onto the foot of my bed. He rolled the bed with me in it out of the room, down the hall, into and then out of the elevator, and then down the most isolated and desolate corridor that must have existed in the hospital, and finally into the operating room.

The operating room was cold and sterile, and the technicians were casual and downright lax. They seemed removed, preoccupied, and insensitive. They moved around me, paying most of their attention to what they were ordering for lunch. Maybe they were used to this procedure, but I wasn't.

Finally, one of the technicians approached my bed and asked me my name. Then he and the escort walked out of the room, leaving me there with no clue as to what was happening. I was scared and alone. I felt I had reason to be.

Tears began to fall from my face, and just as they did, a young woman appeared at my side. Dressed in a technician's coat, she wiped my face and told me not to worry. She proceeded to prep me for the procedure. She changed my robe, put extra blankets and sheets over me, and then identified the area on my chest where the port would be inserted. She began to sterilize the area.

Two other technicians joined her, and together they lifted me off my bed and onto the operating table.

The surgeon then entered the room. He walked right over to me, explained the procedure, prepped himself, and went to work. He gave me an anesthetic. A little more than twenty minutes later, I woke up with tubes dangling from a hole in my chest.

⌣➞

I had a single room, as that was necessary for my recovery. I had a low immune system, rendering me more susceptible to the germs of others, so I couldn't share a room or bathroom with another sick person. Besides, I needed to rest.

My room was basic and bland. The décor was dated with wood paneled walls and a linoleum floor. The furniture consisted of a hospital bed, rolling drawers with a Formica top, and an orange chair that reclined into a lounging chair big enough to sleep in.

Despite being simple and dated, the room felt bright and, at times, cheerful. On the wall next to the bed, Mom had put up pictures of the kids and pictures of Shawn and me. When staff entered the room for the first time, they asked about the kids, which gave me a reason to smile and brag about them. I couldn't show them off in person because they weren't allowed to visit for fear they might be carrying germs, as kids often do without knowing it. There were lots of stuffed animals, books, scarves, and t-shirts and caps with inspirational words that friends and family had brought or mailed to the hospital. Mom and Elsa laid them out on the bench beneath the room's windowsill.

There was also twenty-four-hour company. Shawn and Mommy alternated staying overnight every night, except for when Elsa was in town. She would come into town and spend the night in the hospital as often as she could, keeping me company and giving Shawn and Mom a break. Joyce and my cousin, Leigh, took turns staying with me throughout the day. There were many more visitors who came and left cards, books, and gifts for me, even though they couldn't see me as visitation was still highly restricted. I was never lonely or depressed as I lay in that bed. I was being held up by people who mattered to me—and by the doctors and nurses too.

One day while I lay in the bed, what seemed like the angel of touch appeared. Though I was groggy when Beth, who just happened to be my good friend Jess' mom, entered my room, I saw her clearly. She was beautiful, maybe 5'3", with blond, shoulder length hair, and a small and slender frame. In she walked, holding her CD boom box. Her face and demeanor were youthful, and her body was extremely fit. Her countenance was easy to read. She was gentle yet strong, nurturing but firm, compassionate, and full of conviction. She was on a mission. Her presence felt like it was purposeful. She seemed like an angel sent to bring comfort and healing—not with words but with her hands—to those grappling with the heaviness that is cancer. Beth was a massage therapist who was indeed blessed with the power to heal the heart, mind, and soul with touch. She asked my husband and me if she could give me a foot and leg massage. I initially hesitated, but then I said yes. That day and many others that followed, Beth caressed my legs and feet, causing me to feel peace, at least for the time she was there.

But still, the early days of my journey were rough. Despite the company of those to whom I felt closest, I felt both physical and mental anguish. Besides the uncertainty of whether I would survive cancer, there were the daily spiking fevers that served as reminders of the initial onset of my illness, infections the doctors couldn't explain, the ulcer on my backside that resulted from lying in my own excrement while in a coma, and the red and white blood cell and platelet counts that were all over the place. I learned the frightening way that I couldn't even brush my teeth because with low platelets my gums would bleed. I felt completely out of control.

One Sunday afternoon, Elsa came to visit and together we listened to Daddy's sermon, "Witness in Weakness." Daddy preached, "If we are willing, God can use our weakness . . . When I am weak, then am I strong. My strength is rooted in weakness . . . Turn your weakness over to Him, and His grace will be sufficient. So let weakness witness and testify to the power of God's grace."

It was just the sermon I needed to hear.

CHAPTER
FIVE

Embracing My Reality

October 16, 2009 was the day we learned that preliminary results of tests administered following chemotherapy showed no signs of leukemia.

GOD be praised!

Even though I knew that I wasn't completely out of the woods—that without a bone marrow transplant, my doctors believed I'd suffer a relapse—my joy upon learning the chemotherapy had worked and the cancer cells had been killed was undiminished. In that moment, it was the best news possible.

⌒

I wanted the days to go by quickly. I wanted to get on with it—with cancer, with treatment, with transplant, with life.

It didn't take long to settle into a routine in the hospital. I met the morning with enthusiasm, much like I always had. Like clockwork, sometime around 5:00 AM every morning, I'd wake up and determine there was no use in trying to get good, deep sleep anymore. Constant poking by nurses taking my blood and checking my vitals, medicine-induced insomnia, and anxiety were my constant interruptions. So, I would grab my Bible, which rested on the nightstand next to the head of my hospital bed, and read.

I read the book of Job and I drew inspiration. I read the Psalms, and I gained more faith and assurance. I read books and chapters throughout the Old Testament, and I marveled at what the Lord had promised and what He had delivered.

Shawn or my mom, whoever of the two was on duty with me throughout the night before, would begin stirring, usually around 6:00 AM. As soon as they did, I would turn on the TV and watch the news. I didn't pay much attention to the weather. I wasn't going anywhere.

I'd watch Shawn and Mom prepare to leave me. They would wake up their bodies—which had been curled up in the reclining chair for at least seven hours—by stretching and extending their arms and legs. After several seconds passed, they would jump up as though they had awakened to the realities of the day. They would greet me with a kiss and with the same words every morning: "How do you feel?" I'd smile and say, "Okay." Then they would head off to the bathroom, which was outside of the room and down the hall, to shower and dress.

I secretly hated this time. I wanted them to stay all day, to stay with me. But they couldn't. They had jobs. They had my children to take care of. There was life outside of my hospital room, and they were living theirs.

Every morning we would anxiously await Dr. Halperin's report. Shawn would time his departure to leave after Dr. Halperin made his early morning rounds. We had the same questions for him every day: How are my counts? White and red blood cells, and platelets? Are they high enough? High enough to go home? Any signs of cancer? Am I still in remission? No more infections? No more fevers? How do my lungs sound? Clear, yes? How soon can we get on with the transplant? How soon can I see my children? It took a while for each of my questions to be answered satisfactorily, and each day proved to be a lesson in patience.

Before leaving me, whoever of the two was there would help me get out of bed and take a walk around the hospital floor. Because I had lain in bed for weeks, unable to move around, my muscles were weak and my body was sore. I had to regain my strength and the ability to walk more than a few feet at a time before I could go home. We all were committed to making sure I could walk without difficulty as soon as was feasible.

I would rise slowly, putting one foot on the ground first and then the other. I would put on one of the pretty robes my friends had given me, and take Shawn or Mommy's hand as I struggled to find my balance.

Our first walks were no longer than three or four minutes. I couldn't walk any more than that. I didn't have the energy. But I grew stronger quickly. Perhaps because my body at its core was strong, as the doctors had indicated, or because I was resolute that I wasn't going to be hospitalized any longer than was necessary. I knew that moving around with increasing ease and looking physically able would help me get home sooner. And, in a matter of days, I was doing laps around that hospital floor.

As I walked, I would sneak a peek into the rooms of other patients and I would imagine what their stories were. Every day that I walked around the floor, I saw many of the same people sitting or lying in their beds alone. I wondered if they had friends and family. I saw others with family draping their beds, clinging to them and holding on to the moment, and I imagined that their remaining days weren't many in number. I prayed for them all.

There were two locations along the walk that I looked forward to reaching every time. The first was the big window that provided a view of the street below—a bustling New York City corner. I would stop at the window, stand there, and take in the scene. People coming and going, living their lives. I would imagine myself joining them soon. I also liked looping the nurses' station. Every time I did, the nurses would cheer me on and tell me I was looking good. I desperately needed their encouragement.

Throughout the morning, I watched mind-numbing television shows. I became fixated on the *Kathie Lee and Hoda TODAY* show. I couldn't believe that in 2009, two mature, intelligent, and accomplished women were carrying on like stereotypical Barbie dolls on television, and that they seemed happy about it. Then again, they were getting paid. I would flip channels between them and *Let's Make a Deal* with Wayne Brady. I didn't really enjoy that show either but I like Wayne Brady.

Sometimes all the morning television I endured was strictly the prelude for arguably the greatest game show of all time, *The Price is Right*. I developed an addiction to the show. As I watched, I became both the contestants and the audience, rooting on all the players from the time their names were called, to when they cast their bids, and then as they played and won or lost.

I shared my obsession with a few friends and family, and they were amused. Jen addicted to *The Price is Right*, huh? It wasn't that far-fetched. I was living out my desires for healing and recovery through them. Every time a contestant beat the odds and won, I won, and my hope and belief that I would make the right moves, overcome the odds, and survive this disease that threatened to take me out would increase.

I had the same feeling watching the World Series from my hospital bed. The New York Yankees were in the World Series that year, and even though I'm not a diehard fan of professional baseball, I watched every game. I kept thinking about how in 2001, in the weeks that followed 9/11, the Yankees were in the championship series. It seemed everybody was hoping for a win that would symbolize the resurgence of New York City and America. The Yankees represented the fight and champion in us all. The Yankees didn't win that year, and perhaps many of us who were seeking a win to provide comfort after the terrorist attacks felt a greater sense of despair. But this time, the outcome of the World Series would be different, I thought. If the Yankees won, I would win. I would defeat cancer.

They won.

I pretty much stayed away from the soap operas unless I had company and didn't feel like talking much. Even though I grew up on soaps, running home from school to watch pre-recorded VCR tapings of *General Hospital* and *All My Children*, I now had very little interest in them. Hell, I didn't need them. I was living my own drama.

I napped a lot in the afternoon. When awake, I enjoyed Joyce's and Leigh's company. But all the while, I secretly wished the clock would speed up during the day so I could get to and through another night, and get on with cancer, get on with treatment, and get on with life.

Every day in the midst of all my morning TV watching and afternoon napping, I held court with a slew of doctors and nurses. They came individually and in groups throughout the day to complete their rounds, examining and resolving one new medical occurrence after the next.

There was the infectious diseases specialist who was constantly adjusting the antibiotics I was receiving in an attempt to control for and prevent infection and to counter my body's resistance to a medication he had previously prescribed. There was the dermatologist who had to examine and treat the ulcer on my backside; it was raw and wouldn't heal. There was the allergist who tended to the itchy, painful, hot rash and the swelling all over my body. Both were the result of an allergic reaction to medication I had to take. There was the nurse who treated my hemorrhoids, which were a side effect of the cocktail of medications I was taking. And there was the gynecologist who was brought in to look at and treat my enlarged labia, also the result of medications and being sedentary for too long.

At times, it felt like if it could happen, it was going to happen to me. If there was even the slightest possibility of a side effect tied to a medicine I was taking or a consequence from a procedure I was undergoing, it seemed certain I'd experience it. To say I felt physically miserable would be a gross understatement.

Never to be forgotten, there was a reaction one time to the medicine—the dreadful medicine—that I felt certain was going to end my life. All day long the attending doctors and nurses had been standing over my body and conferring about when I was going to receive the medicine. Ultimately, they decided to give it to me at the end of the day, right before Dr. Halperin left. I had no idea what the medicine actually was and why it was so important that it be timed just right. No idea until the medicine was given to me.

With one injection into the tubes dangling from my port, the medicine entered my body and bloodstream. Instantly, I began shaking uncontrollably, and my heart began racing. It beat so fast I was certain it was going to explode. I just knew that whatever they had given me had sent me into an altered state from which I wouldn't recover. I was going to die, right in that very moment on that hospital bed. I was about to die, and I couldn't do anything about it.

My reaction had been anticipated, and within just minutes the attending physician prescribed a drug to counter it. My body responded immediately and my heart rate slowed down. I recovered quickly from the physical scare. However, the mental and emotional trauma still lingers.

Chapter Five

After days and days of asking, I received the answers I longed to hear from Dr. Halperin: "Yes, your kids can visit. And yes, you should be able to go home in time for Halloween." I was thrilled. I was making progress. "Yes" meant I would soon be getting on with my life.

Upon finally hearing these words from the doctor, I instantly realized that I wasn't ready. I hadn't prepared myself for the fear that would accompany the joy of actually experiencing these two milestone events. *What will my children think when they see me? See me looking frail due to the loss of both muscle and over twenty pounds, and to my skin having been darkened and grayed by the chemo. What will they say? Will they be afraid to touch me? When I go home what will happen? What if I get a fever? What if I can't manage my medicine? What if I die?*

I wrestled with these thoughts. I didn't try to shrug them off. Sometimes I just let them hang in the air while I allowed myself to feel them, to own my worries and my fears. This was my reality, and even if I couldn't control it, I had to embrace it.

The Saturday after Dr. Halperin gave approval for Kennedy and Channing to visit, Shawn drove them into Manhattan to the hospital. Mommy helped me get ready. She helped me change into a pair of lounging pants and a basic cotton top. I put the pretty pink robe that my friend gave me on over my clothes. It was the first time in over a month that I was out of a hospital gown and in regular clothes—clothes that hung on me like I was nothing more than a hanger.

Mommy and I tried together to fix my hair, which had already begun separating from my scalp because of the chemo treatments. Not much we could really do with it. Just two twists that each day were becoming more and more matted.

I looked like a shriveled-up mess, but I had a smile.

When Shawn called and said that he and the kids were close, I filled up with emotion, both joy and anxiety. I was grateful for the opportunity to see my children, to just look at them, but I was scared about how they would react. It had been five weeks since they had come to the hospital to say their goodbyes to me. What would they see and what would they think when they looked at me? Would they stand away from me? Would they be afraid to touch me? Would they let me touch them?

Together they came into the room, Channing first, then Kennedy and then Shawn. Channing—every bit a self-assured seven-year-old—walked right up to me and said in a soft, but firm voice, "Hi Mom." Kennedy—my always graceful, poised, and thoughtful preteen—moved a little more gingerly, somewhat hesitantly. Her eyes, however, dashed all around, attempting to take it all in— the room, the medical equipment, and me. Channing fell right into routine. He began sharing with me his entrepreneurial plan to set up a business where he would sell his second-grade classmates' artwork. It would be easy, he told me. "They like to draw pictures, and so they will draw them, give them to me, and I'll sell them for $2.00 or $2.50 each outside of school at dismissal."

Channing was also excited about Halloween, which was just a little more than a week away. Shawn had told him I might be home by then, and he was anxious for me to see his costume. He was planning to dress up as a ninja!

Kennedy remained quiet, saying only one or two words in response to my questions.

"How's school?"

"Fine," she said.

"Do you like dance this year?"

"Yes."

Perhaps she said more, but I can't recall. I just remember my beautiful twelve-year-old daughter trying not to appear uncomfortable, but all the while looking both anxious and scared.

It wasn't until a year later when Kennedy wrote an insightful essay, expressing the flowerbed of emotions she felt in the first days and weeks of my illness, that I truly understood what she had been feeling:

> *I slept, woke up, and passed through the days emotionless. The vibrancy of my personality drained and the vivid colors all faded to black and white. Conversations blurred and I stumbled through classes, slightly listening to the teachers, catching every seventh word, and then crawling back into the furrow of nothingness. This merciless disease of not knowing what to do clung to every inch of my body and sucked me into an abyss where I just let life happen.*

My mother not being there meant that she did not cook dinner, meant that she was not there to yell at me when I sneaked makeup on my face, meant that I had to adapt. Adapting and change go hand in hand. They skip in the park together always holding hands and hugging. Quite frankly, I was never happy with change unless it benefited me.

I found myself walking blindly with my mother not being around. She guided me on my path and then let me decide things that were not as critical as the decisions she made for me. Without her I had to let go of the notion that my mother will always help me live my life. I had to make decisions that I did not want to make, which caused me to see the world as a despicable and loathsome place to where I was thrust.

The doctor gave me permission to sit with Shawn and the kids in the visitors' room where there were plenty of chairs and tables. As we walked to the room together, I tried to walk as normally as I could. Not so easy. I was weak. Mom stayed back in my room. She said Shawn, the kids, and I should spend a little time together alone—as alone as we could be in a public visitors' room.

We ordered pizza—one of the few foods I could eat from the outside as long as it wasn't cut into slices. I was on a neutropenic diet, which meant that I could only eat foods that likely didn't have bacteria or other harmful organisms that my weakened immune system wouldn't be able to protect me from. An uncut pizza would likely go from the oven to the box without coming in contact with a knife or raw food that might contain bacteria, and thus, it was considered safe to eat. The foods I enjoyed most like fresh fruits and vegetables, as well as raw nuts and yogurt, were on the don't eat list. Raw or rare-cooked meat, fish, and eggs were definitely out of the question. But it wasn't hard to adjust, not when my life depended on it.

The pizza arrived and the four of us sat and ate together rather quietly. We talked, but not a lot. We tried to be as familiar and at ease with each other as we always were, but we could only pretend so much. It was awkward sitting in a public room with other people nearby, trying to mute out the obvious thoughts on all our minds and still experience and feel a true connection.

After a half hour or thereabouts, Shawn announced that it was time to leave. Channing winced a little, but didn't put up a fight. Kennedy said nothing. I wanted more time with them, but Shawn was right. The visit had been long enough.

CHAPTER
SIX

Heading Home

Three days later, I got good news. I was being cleared to go home. My white blood and platelet counts were good, my hemoglobin was good, there were no more fevers, and I was walking well enough.

Before I could go home, though, I had to have another surgical procedure to remove the port that had been placed in my chest just weeks before. I'd complained for several days that the port area was sore. However, the nurses and doctors didn't think anything was wrong because the port was functioning properly. They could extract blood from it and give me medication and infusions through it. But something was wrong, and I insisted they take a look. The technician came to my room and x-rayed my chest, and well, what do you know, there was something wrong—the port was infected and had to be removed.

The next day, I was wheeled back to the operating room I didn't like. Back to the table. Different people, though. The nurse prepped me and knocked me out. I woke up a short while later with a hole 4.5 centimeters wide in my chest.

The surgery wasn't bad, but the healing was. The worst was the day before I left the hospital to come home. My nurse had to clean the wound. It wasn't stitched up. Rather, it was to heal while open—from the inside out. Cleaning required the nurse to pour saline solution in the wound, but first she had to remove the gauze placed in the hole in my chest. And so she commenced to do so, grabbing hold of the gauze to take it out. With her first tug at the gauze, I squealed like a pig. The gauze that had been stuffed in the wound to catch the blood and puss from the infection had dried up and become attached to the flesh of my chest. As the nurse tugged at it, she pulled on my flesh. I screamed and moaned, and she kept pulling and tugging. The pain felt worse than childbirth. And she just kept on.

Mom was there, standing by the side of the bed, holding my hand and crying with me. It was torture.

Eventually, the gauze was out. Every part of it was saturated with dried and fresh blood, and yellowish puss.

The nurse apologized profusely. She had no idea the gauze had been pushed so deeply into my chest. When I think about it today, I can still feel the pain.

On the day I was released from St. Vincent's Hospital, Friday, October 30, my emotions were all over the place. After what seemed an eternity but was only five and a half weeks, I was excited to be going home, to see my children, and to sleep in my own bed. But I was also nervous about what home life would be like. Would we be just as we were as a family before I got sick? Would the kids act differently? Would I?

Shawn arrived at the hospital in time to help me dress. He brought me a pair of jeans and a lightweight sweater. I was glad he did. I didn't want to put on the clothes I was wearing when I entered the hospital weeks before. I secretly believed they held my sickness. I wanted no part of them.

As I put on my bra—the first time I had one on in weeks—I got a real sense of how thin I had become. The straps were loose and the cups twice as big as my breasts. No fat left in them.

My pants were sagging everywhere. As I buttoned them, I looked up and caught Shawn looking at me. I blurted out, "I look like the reverse of Benjamin Button. I've aged overnight!" We broke out in laughter. At least we were the same with each other as we'd always been.

As we prepared to leave, Dr. Halperin stopped by. He wished me well, and then he directed me to make an appointment with Dr. Roboz, the leukemia specialist at New York-Presbyterian Weill Cornell Medical Center with whom he'd been conferring about my case from day one when I was first diagnosed. Together they came up with the treatment regimen that got me through my first near-death battle with leukemia. Dr. Halperin felt it important that I see her, as she is a leukemia specialist, and he is a hematologist. New York-Presbyterian also has a bone marrow transplant practice onsite. I was to see her right away—Monday, if possible.

I quickly surmised that going home didn't mean I was well. It just meant this part of the journey was ending, and the next part was about to begin. As my friend Bernie would later exhort, "Remember, this is a marathon, not a sprint." I called and made an appointment with Dr. Roboz for Monday, November 2 at 11:00 AM.

Heading out of the hospital, we stopped at the nurses' station and I said my goodbyes and thank yous. I remember thinking, *Doctors treat but nurses heal*, for it was the nurses who had wiped my tears, held my hands, and comforted me throughout the day and night. I felt that way even about the nurse who ripped my chest apart.

We visited the ICU. I met the nurses and some of the doctors who cared for me—bathed me in ice when my fevers burned me up, administered chemo while I was in a coma, massaged my limbs, and prayed for me. They looked at me and shook their heads in disbelief. I was going home.

The ride home was strange. I felt like a newborn baby being carried home for the first time. The house had been scrubbed down, and new sheets and new towels had been purchased in preparation for my homecoming. I would be watched round-the-clock. My meals would be prepared for me. I had to get plenty of rest.

The kids weren't there when we arrived. That was good. It gave me time to put my head together and to try to feel comfortable at home. It was hard. I was still sick. The future was uncertain. Was my return home temporary? Should I pretend all was well? I was overwhelmed. I was afraid to be out of the sight and care of the hospital staff. I was afraid to be home.

I climbed into bed and motioned for Shawn to join me. He did, and I rested in his arms and cried. I was grateful to be home but I was scared.

I don't remember the kids that night. I don't remember dinner.

I woke up the next morning at 3:30 AM and couldn't go back to sleep. I got out of bed and made my way down the stairs to the first floor of our home, moving at a snail's pace and holding on to the banister for dear life. It had been just days before when I first attempted walking up and down two, and then three, four, and five steps at the hospital.

Once downstairs, I ventured into the TV room, laid myself down on the couch, and turned on the TV. My plan was to become wrapped up in a movie or something. No such luck. I was too worried and scared. I wasn't able to focus or fall asleep. I just lay there, feeling alone and afraid.

That Saturday, Channing and Kennedy had their regular weekend activities. Channing had a baseball game and Kennedy had dance class. I was eager to go to Channing's game.

Shawn helped Channing put his baseball equipment in the car, and then he helped me get in the front seat. When we arrived at the field, I decided to watch from the car. I was too weak to stand outside with the other parents, and I didn't feel like talking. I just wanted to see Channing, and I could do that from the car.

As soon as the game was over, we took Channing to his school's Halloween party and left him there with friends. He didn't complain that neither one of us was going to the party. He wasn't thinking about us. He wasn't thinking about me.

Chapter Six

Kennedy came home from her dance class and began getting ready for a Halloween party. With pink wings and makeup, she was going to transform herself into a fairy. She asked my mother to do her makeup, but my mother insisted I do it. Kennedy hesitated, but eventually she let me. It took a while. I was weak. But I managed, and then I took her picture. She made a pretty fairy.

A short while later, Kennedy was off to party and trick-or-treat, and then spend the night at a friend's home. Channing, too, was spending the night with a friend.

The next day, per doctor's orders, Shawn took me back to the hospital to the emergency room to have the hole in my chest cleaned and the gauze covering the wound changed. At the hospital, I insisted the nurse give me codeine first to help me relax, and that she saturate the wound and the gauze in it with saline before attempting to remove it. The incident with the nurse ripping the gauze out of my chest was still too fresh. The thought of reliving that experience petrified me. Thankfully, I didn't have to. The codeine and the saline worked.

It was Sunday, November 1, and Marathon Day in New York City. Driving back home from Manhattan, we reached a point shortly after crossing the Brooklyn Bridge where we could drive no farther. The streets were blocked and there were runners—healthy and fit runners— everywhere.

Virtually immobile and short on time because we had to pick Kennedy up from her sleepover and I had to get home and rest, we had to ditch the car, find a garage or parking space on the street, and take the subway. We had no choice.

I was scared. So many people. What if I was too weak to walk? What if I picked up germs on the subway?

Shawn made a plan. We would walk three long blocks slowly, take the train underground one stop, and get off and walk three blocks to a cafe. There I would sit with a warm cup of tea while he traveled another six blocks on foot and picked up Kennedy. He would return with Kennedy to the cafe to get me, and then we would walk back to the train and go one more stop to our neighborhood. It may not seem like a big undertaking, but it was at the time and we both were anxious. I was out in the cold, sick and weak.

Shawn executed his plan perfectly. He moved me cautiously through the streets, guarding me like a hen watching her eggs. I made it home, and just in time to cheer for the American marathon runner and underdog, Meb Keflezighi.

He won. Another good sign.

CHAPTER
SEVEN

The Cancer Club

I wasn't home long before I had to return yet again to the hospital. I was due to see Dr. Roboz Monday, November 2 at New York-Presbyterian in Manhattan.

While I wasn't thrilled about having to go to the hospital just three days after getting out and just a day after having been in the ER to have my wound cleaned, I was anxious to hear what Dr. Roboz had to say.

Going into Manhattan also gave me the opportunity to go to my hairstylist's salon and get my hair cut off. The initiation round of chemo had done its thing—killed the cancer, and severed most of the roots of my hair from my head. After weeks of lying in bed on my back, the two French braids my sisters and Leigh had given me and touched up had become locked and matted. They were like nests sitting atop my head, attached to my scalp by so few hair strands you could count them. When I turned my head, my hair literally shifted and followed. It had to be taken off, and soon. It was a constant, nagging reminder of my situation. I wanted it off.

Shawn and I sat in Dr. Roboz's waiting room, waiting to be called. It was a clinic. There were people from all walks of life. Different races, many languages, and an apparent wide range of incomes. A room full of people who typically otherwise would not be in the same place, maybe not even on the same subway line. But we all were there because we had one thing more unifying than any ethnic, race, or class distinction could ever be: cancer. I remember looking around and thinking, *This is my new group, my new classification, my new club. Cancer.*

After a couple of hours, we were called in to see Dr. Roboz. I was struck immediately by her demeanor. She was confident, she was firm, and she was beautiful.

Dr. Roboz began by reviewing my record with me. She was intimately familiar with my case, having conferred with Dr. Halperin when I was under his daily care at St. Vincent's. Nevertheless, she wanted to go over my case with me to make sure I was clear about my condition.

Dr. Roboz didn't hesitate or hold back. She looked me directly in the face. Her words went something like this: "You have an aggressive form of leukemia. You must have a transplant, and we're going to find you a donor. We have to move aggressively. Until we find a donor, you have to undergo consolidation chemotherapy to keep the cancer cells from growing, and you should have only three consolidation rounds of chemo, or the results will be minimized. We're going to start searching the registry for compatible donors, and we'll test Shawn to see if he's compatible. But while we search, you will need to come in for consolidation treatments to keep the cancer cells from growing. Your first consolidation treatment will begin Sunday, November 15."

Sunday! I screamed in my head. I'd just come home. *Why?*

I guess my face said it all. Dr. Roboz looked me straight in the eyes and continued, saying something along the lines of, "If you want to live, you have to do this." I began tearing up. I started asking questions about statistics. "How long do I have if I don't get a donor? Will the cancer return between treatments?"

I had more questions, but she interrupted me: "Here's how this will work best. Just as I shouldn't hire you as my lawyer and then walk into a courtroom and tell you how to handle my case, you have to let me manage your illness. I am your age and I have a son and daughter the same ages as your children. We have to find you a donor so you can raise your children. We will find you a donor."

And without further questions or thought, I surrendered my case to her. I never consulted another book, website, or friend on treatment or my chances. Always the one to try to manage and plan every aspect of my and my family's lives, I let it all go. I put my trust in her. I put my trust in God. I released that aspect of my journey.

⟡

Six hours later, after walking into the clinic, meeting with Dr. Roboz, lying on the examination table for my second bone marrow biopsy (which was more painful than the first but necessary to determine if the cancer was active again), and getting my chest wound cleaned and new bandages applied, Shawn and I left the hospital. We felt hopeful. We had a plan, and we had a doctor who was determined to do all within her power to keep me alive.

Mommy met us at the hospital entrance, and together we traveled to Hairstyles by Joseph, where Walter, my stylist, was waiting for me. It was Monday, and the salon was closed, but Akemi, one of the salon owners, and Walter opened just for me. They expected me at 11:00 AM; I didn't get there until 4:30 PM. They had waited patiently.

When I arrived, Walter and Akemi immediately embraced me with empathetic hugs. Then, Walter walked me to his styling chair. I sat down and he draped a robe over me. I looked in the mirror at my face and hair, and bit my lip in an attempt to hold back the tears. Walter stepped away to get his tools. I closed my eyes and sat resolute. In just seconds, I would hear the buzzing sound of the electric razor. It would zip across my head and cut the few hairs still connected to my scalp.

Walter began. With my eyes closed, I sat still and listened for the buzz. Walter was working but I heard nothing. I slowly opened my eyes, eager and yet afraid to see what was happening. Sure enough, Walter was sitting on his stool, just as he always does when cutting my hair, and he was cutting. He was *cutting* the sparse strands that were still attached to my scalp. No electric razor! Though it would have been much faster and simpler to just shave me bald, Walter used his shears. He cut slowly with precision and deliberation, just as he always had. I guess as far as Walter was concerned, if I was going to be bald or near bald, my head had to be beautiful, and he had to apply the same care and attention he always had to ensure it would be. It didn't make a difference that there wasn't much he could do because there wasn't much left to work with. What seemed to matter more to Walter was how I felt.

As Walter worked, my mother knelt down and picked up the two matted braids from the floor, which once were my crown and glory, and put them in her purse.

Walter finished cutting the few strands of hair that had remained attached to my scalp, and then he walked me over to the sink. I sat down in the chair in front of the sink and put my head back. Walter turned on the water and shampooed and massaged my scalp three times. He then moisturized it. When he was done, he took me back to his chair, and as I sat down, I saw myself, my officially bald self. I managed a slight smile.

CHAPTER
EIGHT

Purpose

My first week at home, Mom and Joyce took turns staying with me during the day while Shawn was at work and the kids were at school. Friends visited but only for a few minutes at a time. When they called ahead of visiting, Mommy made it clear that I was not to be overtaxed or stressed, and she made sure Joyce delivered the same message. Even my closest friends who traveled a considerable distance to see me, like Kim who came from New Jersey and battled rush hour traffic, were admonished not to stay long. I remember being grateful that Kim understood and wasn't dissuaded from coming.

One week after being released, Friday, November 6, I had to travel to Manhattan again to see Dr. Halperin. Mom drove me in and we met Shawn at the doctor's office. When we arrived, Shawn was already standing outside at the entrance, waiting for us. Mommy stayed in the car as Shawn and I went inside.

As soon as we walked through the door and into the waiting area, we were escorted into Dr. Halperin's office. I remember Dr. Halperin was delighted with my appearance. He told me so repeatedly, as if he couldn't believe I was actually standing there alive in his office. We were all smiles.

Then the conversation took a serious turn. The reason we were there was to discuss the results of the bone marrow match tests conducted on each of my three siblings. Dr. Halperin's face grew somber as he delivered the news. He said, "None of your siblings are a match. Two match each other, but none are a match for you."

He may have said more, but that's all I heard. I thought, *None match, but how?* I'd been told that you're most likely to find a match in someone of the same race and ethnicity. They were my best chance—full-blooded siblings. My eyes filled with tears.

Shawn and Dr. Halperin began discussing half-match options and the bone marrow registry. I really didn't hear them. I knew what they were discussing but I simply couldn't start discussing alternatives. I was in shock. I just *knew* one of my siblings would be a match. Just one. I only needed one.

But no. Not even one.

Shawn and I walked out of the office and looked for Mommy and the car. When we spotted each other, she was just up the block, but still she drove to us. Standing at the passenger side window of the car, Shawn leaned in and gave Mom the news. She was devastated. She couldn't hide her despair no matter how hard she tried. We all were in disbelief.

To break the heaviness, Shawn suggested we find a restaurant and have lunch. Mom agreed but insisted we go alone, just the two of us. She insisted on waiting for us in the car.

Purpose

We walked, somewhat aimlessly, and found a nice Chinese restaurant a few blocks east of Dr. Halperin's office. As we sat down, I took off my coat and hat. The waiter looked at me with a face that read surprise. It took me a second, but then it occurred to me that this was actually the first time I was out publicly since my hair had been taken off. The waiter was surprised by my bald head.

I looked around and realized other people were now glancing at me. I became self-conscious, but in a good way. I began pretending that everyone was looking at me and trying to figure out my story.

Was I sick? Was I someone who liked a bald head as a hairstyle? I was in trendy and artsy Soho in Manhattan. It was possible. And then I thought, *They're all looking at me and wondering if I'm terminal. Maybe.*

Shawn and I sat and ate. We ordered dumplings, General Tso's chicken, and something else. I was still on a neutropenic diet, but it was less restrictive for the time being. As long as the food was cooked and served hot, per doctor's orders, I could eat it. I think we had wine.

Shawn smiled at me, held my hand, and told me not to worry. He knew that was easier said than done.

On Saturday, November 14, the day before I was to go into the hospital for my first consolidation treatment, everyone in the house woke up to Channing's frantic cry. He was hysterical. His pet goldfish had died and he was distraught. He asked why the goldfish died. He wondered what he had done wrong.

81

I hugged Channing tight. I sat down on his bedroom floor and crossed my legs, and motioned to him to join me. Holding Channing in my arms, I began explaining how death works. I said, "God gives each of us, including goldfish, life to help fulfill His purposes, and when we have fulfilled His purposes, He calls us home and we die. Not a second before or a minute later." I continued, "Your goldfish served God's purpose and there was nothing you could have done to keep it alive a second longer. When you have done all that God wants you to do, your life ends, and those who love you have to understand your work was done and it was your time to go home."

Many times since, I've thanked that goldfish for serving its purpose—helping me explain death to a seven-year-old child whose mom, by doctors' accounts, was close to it.

That same day in the afternoon, Shawn and I told the kids I had to go back to the hospital the next day. Kennedy said nothing, but Channing, with sadness in his voice, asked why. We explained that I needed more treatment. He didn't understand, but he accepted the news.

I was the one having the hardest time accepting the news. Why did I have to go back so soon? I'd just gotten home. I wanted normalcy. I wanted my life—our life—just the way it always was.

Later that night, I decided to take a bath. At the hospital, I'd been told a bath would be okay as long as the hole in my chest did not get wet. I ventured into Kennedy's room and asked her if I could use her tub. Deep and wide, with a headrest, the tub in her bathroom would provide the relaxation I was seeking. I prepared myself to hear Kennedy complain about my being in her space. Surprisingly, she didn't. Instead, she offered to wash my back.

Kennedy began running the water to fill the tub. Shawn helped me cover the hole in my chest with gauze and tape. I undressed and carefully stepped over the tub rim and into the bath.

My body was frail. Mostly bones and limp, sagging skin. But Kennedy didn't seem to care. She washed my back, gently stroking it with a wash towel soaked with soap and water. As she knelt behind me, I bent my head down and let my tears fall and blend in with the tub water. The loving touch of my twelve-year-old daughter, who could have easily shunned me, was a blessing filled with emotion I could not contain.

The next morning, Shawn, Mommy, and I decided to go to our family church before heading to the hospital. I looked in my closet for something to wear, something that wouldn't droop on me like clothes on a hanger that's too small. I pulled out a brown, long-sleeved turtleneck sweater, a pair of herringbone pants, and a thick, brown crocheted coat-like sweater that stopped at my knees. Sophisticated, smart, and a master disguise to conceal my very thin body underneath. I considered a hat or a scarf to cover my head, but ultimately decided against it. Frameless glasses with a colorless lip gloss would be it. I was going as me.

We entered the church from the back and headed upstairs, taking one step at a time with me moving only as fast as my weak bones would carry me. We'd decided to come in late and leave right after the sermon to avoid contact with other churchgoers, many of whom were like family. Their hugs and kisses, while desired, could be disastrous to my health. My immune system was still compromised. In addition to being cautious about uncooked and raw foods, I also had to guard myself against the common cold, flu, and viruses that people walk around with, sometimes not even knowing it.

When we sat down in the pew, it was just about preaching time. Reverend Peyton saw us enter the sanctuary and acknowledged our presence. It was Men's Day and there was a guest preacher in the house.

The preacher's sermon was long and I can't recall much of it. However, I do remember him speaking about fatherhood, and one thing in particular. He was talking about how parents worry endlessly about their children when really they shouldn't if they trust God. His exact words were: "Don't you know God's been raising children since the beginning of time?"

All of a sudden, that long-winded preacher with whom I wasn't connecting was talking to me. It was as though he was speaking directly to me, as though he knew my heart and soul, as though he knew my greatest fear. What would happen to my children if I died when they both were still so young? The minister's words were like an answer from on high: my children would be fine because God knows best how to care for His own.

CHAPTER
NINE

Holding Two Truths

I checked into the hospital later that afternoon, and within hours I had a new PICC line (peripherally inserted central catheter) for chemotherapy, drawing blood, and other treatments. Unlike the traumatic procedure I'd endured when the port in my chest—now a hole—was first implanted, the PICC, which dangled from my arm, had been threaded through my arm into a central vein in my chest while I lay in my hospital bed awake with a local anesthesia.

God be praised for the little, yet big, victories.

Within minutes of the PICC line being implanted, my five-day regimen of round-the-clock consolidation chemotherapy began. I had a twelve-hour chemo drip from an IV with six-hour breaks in-between for a saline drip to flush my system. Except for a thirty-minute respite every other day during which the IV tubes for the chemo and saline were replaced, I was hooked up to the IV with a pole and monitor all day every day for five days. I was hooked up even when I showered and when I went to the bathroom.

Dr. Roboz warned Shawn and me that my body might react negatively to the chemotherapy. She told us that I might feel nauseous and fatigued both during and after treatments. But surprisingly, the chemo wasn't bad. I didn't get sick at all. No vomiting. No diarrhea. Nothing.

I often wondered if it was a mind over matter thing. Was I just so thankful to be alive and receiving treatment that I refused to let my body register any negative reactions? It probably wasn't just that, but to think so helped me feel like I had some control.

I woke up every morning around 5:00 AM, just like when I was in the hospital previously. I would reach for my Bible on the nightstand next to my bed and open it up to the Psalms. I mostly focused on Psalms 23 and 27. They were the Psalms that as a youth I memorized in Sunday School, and from that time often returned to for comfort and encouragement, especially when feeling vulnerable.

Psalm 23 (KJV)

1 The Lord is my shepherd; I shall not want.

2 He maketh me to lie down in green pastures: he leadeth me beside the still waters.

3 He restoreth my soul: he leadeth me in the paths of righteousness for his name's sake.

4 Yea, though I walk through the valley of the shadow of death, I will fear no evil: for thou art with me; thy rod and thy staff they comfort me.

5 Thou preparest a table before me in the presence of mine enemies: thou anointest my head with oil; my cup runneth over.

6 Surely goodness and mercy shall follow me all the days of my life: and I will dwell in the house of the Lord for ever.

Psalm 27 (KJV)

1 The Lord is my light and my salvation; whom shall I fear? The Lord is the strength of my life; of whom shall I be afraid?

2 When the wicked, even mine enemies and my foes, came upon me to eat up my flesh, they stumbled and fell.

3 Though an host should encamp against me, my heart shall not fear: though war should rise against me, in this will I be confident.

4 One thing have I desired of the Lord, that will I seek after; that I may dwell in the house of the Lord all the days of my life, to behold the beauty of the Lord, and to inquire in his temple.

5 For in the time of trouble he shall hide me in his pavilion: in the secret of his tabernacle shall he hide me; he shall set me up upon a rock.

6 And now shall mine head be lifted up above mine enemies round about me: therefore will I offer in his tabernacle sacrifices of joy; I will sing, yea, I will sing praises unto the Lord.

7 Hear, O Lord, when I cry with my voice: have mercy also upon me, and answer me.

8 When thou saidst, Seek ye my face; my heart said unto thee, Thy face, Lord, will I seek.

9 Hide not thy face far from me; put not thy servant away in anger: thou hast been my help; leave me not, neither forsake me, O God of my salvation.

10 When my father and my mother forsake me, then the Lord will take me up.

11 Teach me thy way, O Lord, and lead me in a plain path, because of mine enemies.

12 Deliver me not over unto the will of mine enemies: for false witnesses are risen up against me, and such as breathe out cruelty.

13 I had fainted, unless I had believed to see the goodness of the Lord in the land of the living.

14 Wait on the Lord: be of good courage, and he shall strengthen thine heart: wait, I say, on the Lord.

After reading the scriptures, I would stretch my arms and back, plant my feet on the cold linoleum floor, and reach for my robe in the chair next to the nightstand by my bed. Maneuvering the IV tubes through my robe sleeve, I would put on my robe. Seconds later I would be out my hospital room door and walking the hospital floor for exercise, both mental and physical.

With my iPod shuffle clipped to my robe lapel, my walking companions were my gospel friends and songs, including Marvin Sapp's "Praise Him in Advance," DeWayne Woods' "Let Go, Let God," Bebe and Cece Winans' "In the Meantime," and Donnie McClurkin's "Didn't You Know." I listened to them over and over, repeating one song five or six times before moving on to the next.

As I walked and listened, my spirit soared. I sensed victory. I felt like I was somehow both in and yet beyond my situation, like the cancer was a part of my life journey but not my entire journey. I felt like I was going through something, a big something, but that something was not how my life would be defined. I felt like there was so much more to me, and the cancer just added another dimension.

I traveled the same route every morning. Once out of my room I'd make a right turn. Within twenty-five feet stood the west nurses' station. I'd circle it and head to the north corridor, which led to the guest elevators. Bypassing the elevators, I'd make two left turns and head down the south corridor. At its end, I would make a right turn and head toward the east nurses' station and the bone marrow transplant unit.

I never stopped at the double doors leading to the bone marrow transplant unit or attempted to walk through them. The unit was restricted to medical personnel, and transplant patients and their families. But as soon as the doors were within view, I said a prayer and I told myself that indeed, I would be a patient in that ward and that I would receive a transplant.

I tried hard to envision myself on the other side of the double doors undergoing transplant, but it never worked. I did believe the Lord would make a way and that I would receive a transplant, but I really wasn't able to place myself in the ward. I told myself that because I couldn't see past the unit doors, I couldn't envision the space and myself in it. Doubt sometimes crept into my mind. Maybe I couldn't visualize myself in the ward because I wouldn't get a transplant.

Turning left just as I neared the transplant unit, I'd circle the east nurses' station, head west toward my room, and once there, repeat the route several more times.

Every morning after completing my walk, I visited the patients' lounge. It was always empty at that time of day, and it was the only place I could truly be alone. There I sat by myself and prayed and read more of the Bible.

During those moments in the lounge in the quietness that accompanied the dawn of the new day, I would shut out the world completely, even if just for a few minutes, and live completely in my reality. I began writing as a way of sharing the thoughts I just couldn't keep in my head:

> *I may die sooner, much sooner, than I had hoped and planned. My desire for more days, many more days, might not be consistent with God's will. And if so, I have to accept and embrace that reality in order to have peace, and to help my children and husband and my family find peace.*

I prayed that my desires would be consistent with God's will, and then I planned in case they weren't. I sketched out my funeral program in my journal, just in case. I wrote my feelings about death and dying:

When My Time Comes

> *Most of us know neither the day nor the hour when we shall lay down and die and move from this place to our place of rest. Having cancer can make this uncertainty a very real and immediate concern for individuals so afflicted and those in their camp.*

> *The question—Am I going to die?—looms large in the mind and heart. Just contemplating death is a*

heavy subject, but then when thoughts concerning the life you may leave behind and the well-being of those you love enter and dominate the emotional, spiritual, and physical debate, the question can become all-consuming—a part of every conversation and most thoughts, spoken and unspoken.

Responses to my examination of the question have varied significantly. Both joy and fear have abounded, sometimes simultaneously. For those I have engaged in this examination, in this personal and emotional self-assessment, the responses have covered the full spectrum of emotion, evidencing different coping levels along the scale of the human's ability to deal with mortality. For some, the conversation is openly welcome—a necessary conversation. For others, it's a taboo subject because, well because, "You're not going anywhere."

Being a planner and a firm believer in the will of God and the constant beneficiary of His good and perfect love, the question and the consequential conversations and internal debates it stirs up are par for the course, and wholly consonant with who I am, the authentic me. To not question or to not openly contemplate the world without little old me would be counterintuitive, a complete contradiction of who I am and what I believe—that the will of God is at all times the decisive and most perfect determinant, and that my purpose has been and is to be at peace with His will, and live and die accordingly.

So to contemplate the future and an earlier than desired death is not to doubt God's grace, mercy, and ability to do all things, but rather to be accepting and at peace with what may be His will—to live with faith, hope, and the belief that God will give me more days on this earth if that is His will, but also to know that "For me to live is Christ, and to die is gain" (Philippians 1:21, KJV).

When my time comes, I hope somebody will say, "She sought to fulfill His purpose, and to love and be loved. Her life was full of love, and it ended when His purpose for her was fulfilled. She thanked God for her journey, every part of it."

Two days into the consolidation chemotherapy treatment, the transplant doctor came to see and talk with Shawn and me. She told us that her office had activated the search for a donor for me, and would be running my human leukocyte antigen (HLA) typing against worldwide bone marrow donor registries with as many as eight million registered persons. She added that she didn't know how long it would take for the results. HLA typing is a blood test performed in anticipation of transplant to learn if a possible donor and donee's body tissues are compatible and if their blood cells match.

Shawn asked her if we should begin organizing donor drives, like the one for the little girl I'd heard about when riding home from work in the taxi cab just weeks before. He wanted to register potential donors should there not already be a match in the registries for me. The doctor said no.

We were shocked.

She unequivocally said *no.*

I don't clearly remember all that she told us after that but I do remember her saying that if there wasn't already a match in the registry for me, donor drives most likely wouldn't make a difference. She seemed confident that a handful of community drives weren't going to increase the pool of registered persons enough to materially increase my likelihood of finding a donor. She said we shouldn't spend our time being frantic with drives, but rather, we should focus on being mentally and emotionally strong for the next phase of our ordeal, whatever that looked like.

We were astounded. How could we not do drives? Wasn't a transplant my only hope? What if there wasn't a match already? Could we risk not trying to find that one person? What if I died and we had not tried?

Shawn and I attempted to stay focused and to continue listening to the doctor. She said something about haploidentical (haplo) matches, which are half matches when you don't have a perfect match. She said something about the success rate for haplo matches getting better. We heard what she was saying and I guess we understood where she was coming from, but it was hard to focus.

When the doctor left, I turned to Shawn and asked him his opinion about donor drives. Always one to be driven by pragmatism and not emotion, Shawn responded without hesitating. "We're doing drives," he said.

We were pressing forward, full steam ahead. We were going to do all we could. We were determined to find me a match, and matches for others, too.

CHAPTER
TEN

Chosen

The initial consolidation treatment went well, and I was released on Friday, November 19. I would be home for Thanksgiving, which was just six days away. My counts were low and I'd have to watch what I ate—like uncooked greens or cooked dishes that sat out too long—to avoid bacteria-related illnesses. That didn't bother me though. All that mattered was that I'd be home.

The next day, I made an effort to resume normalcy in my life. I moved around Brooklyn in the car with Shawn, shuttling the children to and from their weekend activities. After dropping Kennedy at dance class, Shawn and I rushed to a Verizon store to purchase a new phone for her. Kennedy's phone had truly seen its last days weeks before.

While waiting for her new phone to be activated, I suddenly became very tired. I had to sit down. My mouth tasted of iron. I pulled out a mirror and looked inside my mouth, and I was shocked by what I saw. Little blisters of blood everywhere. On my lips and gums, and on the inside of my cheeks. I was freaked out and scared. What now?

I immediately called the hospital and talked with the attending oncologist on duty. As I described to her the appearance of my mouth and sudden fatigue, she read my charts and learned that I'd just been released after having undergone consolidation chemotherapy. Quickly she put two and two together. My immune system had been wiped out by the chemotherapy, and my counts were low. The blood blisters were a symptom of low platelets. She told me I needed to come to the hospital immediately for a platelet transfusion. She said it wouldn't take long, and that I would be back home in just a few hours.

Shawn and I got the replacement phone and left the Verizon store. We picked up Kennedy from dance and dropped her off at home. Then we headed into Manhattan to the hospital.

We arrived at the hospital in the late afternoon to an emergency room filled with people waiting to be seen. I became anxious remembering that I wasn't supposed to be around other sick people, and I became impatient as I didn't want to be there. Then I remembered that in my wallet was a little yellow card Dr. Roboz gave me in the event I needed to come to the emergency room— the cancer card. Flashing the card would expedite my triage and treatment. I whipped it out, and it worked immediately. I was triaged within minutes.

The over-the-phone diagnosis was confirmed. My platelets were too low. I needed a transfusion. The attending physician ordered platelets from the nearby blood bank and an x-ray of my chest to ensure my PICC line was clear and functioning properly.

They moved quickly. I had an x-ray and then I was placed in a private room in the ER to be hooked up to an IV to receive the platelets through my PICC line. *It won't be long,* I thought. I imagined I would receive the platelet transfusion, and then shortly after, Shawn and I would be on our way home.

Hours passed.

Nothing.

I had an eerie feeling there was a reason for the holdup, especially because no one in the ER was communicating with us. I felt no worse than when I first arrived at the hospital and it was confirmed that my problem was low platelets and all I needed was a transfusion, but because they weren't transfusing me and because they weren't telling me anything I began to wonder and worry what was really the matter.

At 2:00 AM, I found out. When the x-ray of my chest was reviewed, the radiologist saw a cavity in my lung. Concerned that it could be tuberculosis, the attending physician gave me a TB test and ordered that I be quarantined in the ER until the results came back. They didn't want me to infect anyone if indeed I had tuberculosis and was in the contagious phase. The doctor said it would take several days to get the results.

I was devastated. I wasn't supposed to be staying overnight—much less possibly days—in the hospital! I wasn't sick. I just came to the hospital to get platelets. The physician on call told me over the phone that I would be in and out of the emergency room. They would give me platelets and I would be on my way. Now they were threatening to keep me, possibly through Thanksgiving.

Silly me. Did I really think I could come to the hospital, be treated, and go home the same day? Really?

Around 6:00 AM, Shawn left the hospital and went home to get some much-needed rest. He'd sat up in a straight back, wooden chair with me all night, dozing off occasionally for just minutes at a time.

I was placed in a small room in the ER with a big, heavy metal door that had a sign taped on the outside that read: "Quarantine. Yellow robe, mask, and gloves required." Inside the room there was a bed, a private bathroom, and a clock. No TV. No radio. No phone. No books.

As for that cavity showing up on the x-ray—no big deal. Well, not something the ER staff had to be overly concerned about at that moment, and I told them so. Doctors at St. Vincent's had already discovered it weeks before when I was first hospitalized. Details about the cavity were in my medical records that were transferred from St. Vincent's to New York-Presbyterian. It wasn't tuberculosis. All the doctors had to do was check the record.

The chief pulmonologist, who happened to be a tall, young-looking black man, came to see and talk with me. He brought along his team. He introduced himself, and then he told me that he was going to perform both an endoscopy and a biopsy on the cavity to see what it was.

What?

Hearing his words, I was ready to pounce on him, to scream at him for holding me prisoner and for even suggesting that he might go down my throat and torture me again with an endoscopy when all he had to do was read my record. But I didn't want to rip on him in front of his team. He was a young black man in medicine. I was certain he already had experienced more than his fair share of being ripped.

So I called upon my gentle but firm voice. With the calmest tone I could manage, I explained that the cavity on my lung had already been discovered during my stay at St. Vincent's, that an endoscopy had already been performed, and that the cavity had been biopsied. I told the young doctor that nothing had been found. I then pleaded with him to check my records. I urged him to call Dr. Roboz and Dr. Halperin.

"I'll see what we can do," was all he said. And then he left my room.

There I was, held up in solitary confinement. I'd come for platelets—an in-and-out procedure. But instead I was being held captive in a room with nothing but a bed, a chair, and a clock. In my mind, I was being held hostage for no reason, for had they checked my records or talked with my doctors, they would have known that I didn't have tuberculosis and the cavity had already been discovered and was being monitored. Of course, I understood that in their minds they had good reason, but that didn't lessen my frustration.

Chapter Ten

That Sunday was the longest day. Shawn was running around with the kids, and Mom had a cold so she couldn't come to the hospital and keep me company. I was all alone. Just me and the clock on the wall.

The clock was the basic type that hangs in lots of public spaces. Round with a white face and black hands and numbers.

I stared at the clock and began studying it. I watched the second hand go around the face of the clock over and over. I watched the long hand move slowly between the numbers that represented the hours. And I watched the short hand move ever more slowly. Round and round the second hand went, with the long hand moving only after the second hand seemed like it should have given way due to exhaustion. Watching the short hand rotate was like watching molasses drip.

All of a sudden, it hit me! I was watching the pecking order of society. The clock is a symbol of our society. The second hand passes time and makes sure time never stands still, but it is rarely talked about or paid attention to. The second hand is constantly working but gets little to no respect. Just like the misperception of the lowest man on the totem pole, it's the one that does the bulk of the work and gets the least credit. Then there's the long hand that measures time by minutes. It's like the manager who comes in, sees the good work that's been done, puts his stamp on it, and then takes the credit for having met the goals set. And finally, the short hand, or the hour hand, is just like the boss. It does very little sweat labor and very little grunt work. Yet it takes all the glory for the big outcome—the turning of the hour.

I spent all day Sunday in isolation. With nothing other than the clock to focus on, I grew more anxious and angry. I didn't need to be there. Thanksgiving was just a few days away and they were threatening to keep me in the hospital. Test results would take days, and treatment even longer. All these precautions when all they had to do was check my records. With no one there to advocate for me, to press the doctors, I felt like I was being set back.

And then the Lord sent me a comforter in the form of a complete stranger. As I lay quarantined in that hospital bed, a nurse of Indian descent, petite in size and gentle in her appearance and demeanor, came in to check my vitals. Appearing to be making small talk just to be polite, she asked me about my battle with cancer.

As I shared my harrowing ordeal, she looked directly in my face and said, "Oh, how blessed you are. He chose you."

She continued, "God needed people to receive a message, and He chose you to help them see it, hear it, and receive it."

No doubt, she was sent to remind me that there was purpose in my journey.

Monday came and my doctors were back at work. With Dr. Roboz and Dr. Halperin physically present in their respective hospitals, I prayed something would happen and I'd be set free. I hoped they would just read my records.

By mid-morning, Dr. Roboz appeared. She had reviewed my records with the ER physicians and specialists and convinced them that there was nothing on my lungs that hadn't been detected and analyzed before. There was no reason to keep me in the hospital any longer. She told me I would be released Tuesday afternoon, and she made sure that happened.

On Wednesday, the day before Thanksgiving, I was home with Kennedy and Channing. I felt good enough to cook some of their holiday favorites. I made corn pudding and sweet potatoes, just the way they like them. Lots of butter and sugar. I elected not to cook collards, for that would have been a lot of work and I didn't have the energy.

That afternoon an angel disguised as a visiting nurse came to the house. He was there to change my PICC line tubes and to teach my family and me how to flush the lines to prevent infection between chemotherapy treatments.

I met Anthony in the foyer of our home. I greeted him at the bottom of the front hall staircase and walked with him into the family room. We sat on the couch and he proceeded to ask me a seemingly never-ending series of questions. Many of Anthony's questions felt very personal but he knew just how to make me feel at ease. He'd ask a question, I'd answer, and he'd follow with a relevant and equally personal story of his own, helping me to feel safe and understood.

Thirty minutes later, Anthony had slipped under the veil. Somehow, he'd managed to get around the facade I'd erected for both strangers and friends. He was inside the gate. Anthony connected immediately with my soul. By his words, I knew he understood my fears without me articulating them. I knew he had embraced my desire to just be happy and worry-free. And I knew he was committed to helping me along my journey. I felt that despite my state and what I was up against, he truly believed I would survive. That was all I needed, a stranger who believed in me.

Anthony was fighting his own battles—the tragic loss of his partner, a new relationship that had more than its fair share of challenges, and a desire for true love. Through our mutual sharing, we were able to be a lifeline to each other. We encouraged each other. I prayed for him, and he prayed for me.

On Thanksgiving Day, my heart was full of joy. I was home and my family—Shawn and the kids, my mom, sisters, brother-in-law, and cousin—was with me. We all felt especially grateful. Just weeks before as I lay in a coma, they were grappling with the reality that I might not see Thanksgiving. Our hearts were glad.

Our hearts were also heavy. We knew that if I didn't receive a transplant, this Thanksgiving might very well be my last. So we immersed ourselves in the moment as best we could. We smiled, we laughed, we prayed, and we repeatedly expressed our thankfulness for each other with words, hugs, and kisses. We made the most of our time together.

CHAPTER
ELEVEN

Putting My Story Out There

The Friday after Thanksgiving, Shawn, Mom, Lesley, and Elsa began planning our donor drive strategy. Shawn had made contact with NMDP, the National Marrow Donor Program. In turn, they had put him in touch with Airam da Silva, President of the Icla da Silva Foundation, a local bone marrow donor recruitment organization and an affiliate of NMDP. Shawn had an initial conversation with Airam and told him we were planning to mount an aggressive donor campaign to bring as many as people as were necessary to the registry to find me a donor. Airam cautioned Shawn, gently advising him to lower his expectations because it isn't easy to get people to sign up, let alone actually donate, when called upon to do so. Shawn responded by telling Airam that he should prepare for a major effort because that was what he was planning.

Shawn and I talked about my participation in the drives and the planning, and how involved I should be. We agreed that other than participating in media stories and engaging with NMDP to develop and support outreach campaigns with social and religious organizations of color, I didn't need to be involved. I don't remember Shawn's reasoning, but I remember thinking it would be too much of an added emotional weight if I was tracking every drive scheduled, counting every registrant, and hearing the daily challenges. I was content to provide input only when asked. Sitting on the sidelines was a new role for me, but I didn't reject it.

Three days later, on a Monday evening, Shawn held his first conference call with our family and friends. Just about every region of the country was represented on the call with people from California, Georgia, Connecticut, Virginia, Kentucky, Michigan, Massachusetts, Maryland, New Jersey, New York, North Carolina, Ohio, Tennessee, and Washington, D.C. Shawn described my condition and the urgent need for a donor to be found. He told them my best chance for a match would likely come from someone of similar race and ethnicity—a person of African descent. He asked those on the call for help in setting up drives in churches and community centers, on college campuses, and in workplaces. Before the call ended, all pledged their support and vowed to get to work immediately.

Within days, the team had a flyer with my picture and story on it, a website titled "savejenaustin", and the first drives scheduled. I quickly learned the added value of having a posse of Type A friends.

Saturday, December 5 was our wedding anniversary. Shawn took off Friday, the day before, just as we both had done for several years since having kids so we could spend the day together. We started our day by shopping for Christmas gifts for our nieces and nephews. We went to Banana Republic and Gap, and at both stores I weighed our arms down with sweaters and shirts, dresses and pants. Doing so felt normal, and Shawn just went along with me. Perhaps it wasn't how he wanted to spend the morning, but he didn't complain. We had a hot and hearty lunch at Blue Smoke replete with ribs, mac and cheese, collards, and love. Lots of love.

That afternoon we bought a Christmas tree, and Shawn put it up in the living room. On Sunday, Channing, Kennedy, and I decorated it.

I felt good enough to do it all.

⌒

The first bone marrow donor drive was held on Saturday, December 6, 2009 at the National Action Network's Headquarters in Harlem. Reverend Al Sharpton led the way, swabbing his cheeks to be tested as a potential match for me. Since he was a teenager in the late 1960s, when his mother asked my father to watch over and steer him as he entered the Civil Rights Movement, Rev. Sharpton has been like family. So when Mom called and asked him to host a drive, he didn't hesitate. He opened up the National Action Network House of Justice to us and got the news cameras there to help spread the word.

The next day, Sunday, there were drives in a few churches across the country. In New York City, Reverend Calvin Butts, a family friend and pastor of the Abyssinian Baptist Church in Harlem, opened the doors of the church and community members lined up. Shawn, Anne, and another dear friend, Saadia, were on hand to help. NBC news anchor Melissa Russo and her camera crew captured this event.

Lesley held drives in a few churches in the Cleveland, Ohio community.

Altogether, the first drives brought in over four hundred new donors. We were off to a tremendous start.

Chapter Eleven

While still at Abyssinian Church at the drive, Shawn called to tell me that Melissa Russo was on her way to our house. She wanted to film me for a feature piece to air on NBC to help our drive efforts.

Whoa! Going on television to plead for a donor! Whoa! Did I really want to be seen on television looking the way I did? I was bald and frail. I wasn't prepared.

Just as I was debating with myself whether I should go on camera or instead have Mom answer the door and tell Melissa I wasn't up for an interview when she rang the bell, my phone rang. It was Gail, my friend who always tells it like it is. I shared my angst with her, and in true Gail form, she lovingly shut me down. Gail said, "Do you want to live? Well, if you do, you're going to have to put your story out there."

I hung up the phone and went to my closet to find something to wear.

What fits? What is the look of a woman over forty with cancer?

I didn't have long to think about it, so I just threw on a pair of black knit pants, a black short-sleeved knit top, and some blush, mascara, and lip gloss. My accessories were a dangling PICC line and a bald head. That was it. There wasn't much I could do.

Turns out I didn't need much. The story of my battle and my desire to find a donor and live was enough of an attention-getter. I went on the air and shared my first days and weeks with cancer—the flu-like fever, the diagnosis, the initial treatment, the need for a match, my fears, and just in case I didn't beat it, my plans to complete my babies' photo scrapbooks I'd been working on for years.

I was scheduled to return to the hospital for my second round of consolidation chemotherapy on Monday, December 14. I'd negotiated that date with Dr. Roboz to be sure I could attend Channing's eighth birthday party the weekend before. I had designed, created, and mailed his invitations in November. I had every intention of being there. After all, it was a real possibility this would be the last time I celebrated his birthday.

On Saturday, December 12, we had a birthday party for Channing, teeming with more boys than I could keep track of, pizza and cake, and parents, friends, and family all intent on making the event the happiest occasion. I helped Channing blow out his candles.

That same evening, the NBC news story about my need for a donor aired. Later that night, Shawn got an email from a dear friend who had seen the story. The email read, "Jen might look hotter bald than she does with hair!"

CHAPTER
TWELVE

Should I Die

Sunday came, and Shawn and I returned to New York-Presbyterian Weill Cornell Medical Center for my second round of consolidation chemo.

This time I was ready for my stay. Joyce had given me two sets of pajamas—one set consisted of a solid red top and matching plaid drawstring pants. The other set was green with a solid top, and green on the bottom with white snowflakes. I was ready for the winter and for the holidays.

I brought my scrapbooks with me to make sure I finished them before Christmas, a box of stationery to write keepsake letters to my family and friends, and two special boxes of stationery to write letters to my Kennedy and my Channing. I wanted them to have letters covering a variety of everyday issues and experiences, letters they would turn to and read time and time again should I die and not be there to listen and talk. Most were letters written to both of them, and a few were written specifically for each of them.

On God and Religion

God loves you most. He gave you life and purpose. He is the source of your strength and your joy.

He is your anchor. Cling to Him. He's ALWAYS got your back! He wants you to come to Him for comfort and guidance.

Always remember, life may not go as you plan, troubles may linger, losses and pains may last a lifetime. But in God, you will find the strength to go forward and be victorious. Trust Him with your life. He will not fail you.

Stay in church. It's our stabilizing base here on this earth. Seek the church and fellowship in both good and bad times.

Pray and pray often. It works! Sometimes He answers as we desire and sometimes He answers differently. Just remember, His plan is for you to prosper, even in the midst of pain and disappointment.

God loves you and needs you to survive and thrive.

With Him All Things Are Possible.

Love,

Mommy

On Sex and Sexuality

Extremely overrated when you're young—don't fall prey to the pressures of boyfriends and girlfriends. Losing your virginity to please another does not make you a woman or man, or a grown-up, and you won't feel good in the long run. Trust me!

Sex is beautiful when you're mature in age and mind.

Sex won't help you get or hold on to anyone. Don't let anyone mess with your mind in this way.

Safe sex always—whomever, whatever, whenever! Seek guidance and don't be fooled. Sex can kill or hurt even if it's with someone you're committing yourself to. Oral sex included! Be cautious! Protect yourself and your life!

Sexuality—it's increasingly complicated. Walk the path God has chosen for you.

I love you,

Mommy

On Success

Success is not just what you've done; what's just as important is what you've overcome.

I've heard it said, "They don't write books about people who don't take risks."

You have to prepare for success—mentally, emotionally, physically, and spiritually. It doesn't just happen. Education is key.

Seek knowledge at all times and in all things. Excelling in knowledge is a gift you can give yourself.

Don't throw away your blessings—He's given you many gifts.

As my daddy used to say, "A setback is a setup for a comeback." We fall down and we get back up. God's in the business of redemption and rebuilding. He can do all things exceedingly abundantly.

Work to be the best you can be, and success will come. Perhaps not right away, but it will come.

Ride the bumps. There's reward on the other side.

Proud of you!

Mommy

On Being Black

Be Proud! Be Bold! Be True!

Learn your heritage and be proud of it!

The world has changed much since the days of slavery and the days of legal discrimination, but never be fooled. There still are challenges and dangers you may face simply because you're black. But don't worry. Pray, be smart, be careful, and be thoughtful. Pick your battles wisely.

God will watch over you and you will prosper.

I love you,

Mommy

On Community

Always remember that we are only as strong as our community.

114

You can amass all the wealth and fame this world holds, but if you deny yourself the joy and reward of helping another, your life will feel and be meaningless.

Be humble and help others.

". . . For unto whomsoever much is given, of him shall be much required: and to whom men have committed much, of him they will ask the more" (Luke 12:48, KJV).

Proud of my babies!

Mommy

On Dating and Hanging Out

Have Fun! Don't take it too seriously. Not every date is a marriage prospect, especially when you're young! However, when you're older and mature, if he or she really seems worthy and right for you, then go slow and don't let on too soon that you're thinking such thoughts.

Be careful!!! Not every cute guy or girl is a good guy or girl. Many girls and women have been brutally and fatally harmed by the cute guy. Same with girls harming guys.

Choose to be alone with a guy only when you have used your best judgment. Rape happens more often than you may think.

Always carry "get home" cab money and your phone.

Remember: you can always call your family to pick

you up wherever you are. No questions asked.

Always listen to what people say and do. Do not reduce your standards.

Love you,

Mommy

On the Right Clothes

Whatever the style or trend, keep it smart and keep it clean!

Classic, quality clothes cost more but pay for themselves over time.

We all can't wear everything. Some fashion trends you may have to sit out.

Less says more. Subtle is sexier than letting it all hang out!

Kennedy, wash your bras by hand, and remember that the wrong undergarment can kill an otherwise great outfit. Always have good fitting bras and underwear.

Cheap can make you look cheap.

Black undergarments with black clothes is a good rule.

Love,

Mommy

On *Womanhood*

Always remember your grandmother's words: "Get your degrees before you get married. Have as many children as you want because they are yours to raise. And keep yourself looking good because you never know."

Walk with integrity—seek to do good and to be honest with yourself and those with whom you interact.

Be strong—you have a voice, you have a powerful mind, and you have a right to your opinion.

Be a lady—don't cheapen yourself with cheap or suggestive clothes, or acts of desperation for any guy or girlfriend. You won't feel good in the long run. And clean up after yourself. Your surroundings are a reflection of you.

I love you,

Mommy

On *Family*

Love family always, even when it's hard.

Stay close to them, and remember they need you even when they say they don't.

Be good to your family. Support them in their dreams, and help them when you can.

Keep family traditions. They will be sources of joy when you need comfort and when you need to remember.

Try to be the one to add joy as only you can do!

I love you my sweethearts!

Mommy

I found the letter writing—more than fifty in total—comforting. It was the one thing over which I had real control. Embracing both the lawyer and mommy in me, I was planning concurrently, or perhaps contingently. Even though I had every intention of living, I was writing letters just in case I didn't make it. No one knew I was writing them. I kept quiet about it so no one would tell me not to think this way. No one would try to stop me if no one knew about them.

The chemo treatments proved to not be the hardest part of my hospital stays. Rather, having other people care for my children as if they were their own was what was most difficult. I shall never forget Saturday, December 19, 2009, the night Kennedy went to her first teen party. It was her classmate's bar mitzvah. I'd shopped and bought an outfit for her the day I went Christmas shopping with Shawn, so I felt I had dressed her. But it was her first dance and someone had to do her hair, and it wouldn't be me.

Kennedy wanted to wear her naturally curly and long tresses straight. Mommy was planning to flat iron her hair and I was prepared for Mommy to do that. But then I got a call from Mommy. She had learned that Kennedy had called my cousin, Robin, and asked for her help. The two had made plans. Robin was going to pick Kennedy up from dance class later that afternoon and bring her home and help her get ready for the party.

Not the plan I had put in place, but okay, I thought. For years Robin and Leigh had lovingly cultivated very special relationships with Kennedy and Channing, and now we were experiencing one of the many benefits.

What wasn't okay was what Mommy said next. She told me that Kennedy had asked Robin to take her shopping for new bras. Mommy thought I should know.

We hung up the phone, and I called Shawn immediately. I pleaded with him to tell Robin there was no need for her to take my baby girl shopping for a bra. Kennedy had bras, and if she needed a new one she could wait a few days for me to come home and take her myself. I was prepared to argue my case to Shawn but I didn't have to. He got it right away and said he'd take care of it. He seemed upset that I'd been made upset.

Robin and Mommy both meant well, as did everyone else who was trying to help fill the void created by my illness. The fact was, my children needed a mommy and I wasn't able to meet their needs. It was a painful truth, and I wasn't ready to own it. As far as I was concerned, I was their mommy and would be their mommy— at least until God said otherwise. But my health circumstances weren't allowing me to be the hands-on mother they needed.

I felt like I was losing all control. I had no say in my children's comings and goings. I had no say about what was happening in my home. I had no say in the organization where I'd been working. Even the people who were closest to me and simply trying to help me felt like a threat at times. In doing all they could to meet my children's needs, they were being the mommy I couldn't be.

I had a hard time expressing these feelings because I didn't want my family and friends to think I wasn't grateful. It wasn't easy having others do the things I should have been doing for my children, but I had no choice. I had to relinquish my daily parenting responsibilities. I had little control, and I had to accept that. So I tried not to dwell on it or to share my feelings because when I tried, I wound up sounding emotional and erratic. So instead I wrote:

I'm Here Until I'm Not Here

I need you to help, not take over.

I need you to put my needs first, not your own.

I need you to be sensitive to my feelings and not give in to your own desires.

I need you to respect my roles as wife and mother, and not disregard them.

I need you to let me live my life, and not take it from me.

I need you to love and do for me with acute sensitivity to my situation because love without sensitivity doesn't work for me.

CHAPTER
THIRTEEN

#SaveJenAustin

I got out of the hospital Monday, December 21, just in time to celebrate Channing's actual birthday that day, and then Christmas and New Year's. All were joyous occasions filled with love, memory-making, and lots of picture-taking.

Everyone came home for a few days. Mommy, Lesley and her husband Randy, and Elsa and her children, Brian and Natalia, were there. Billy and his kids, Bill, Justice, and Brooklyn, were home too. We played games, watched movies, and just sat around and talked. Nothing over-planned or overtaxing. Just time together, enjoying each other. The holidays were as close to perfect as they could be. If they were to be my last, we all seemed intent on making sure they were memorable for all the right reasons.

The donor drives continued, and by Christmas, my family, friends, and colleagues had orchestrated over thirty drives and helped register more than 4,000 people as potential bone marrow donors. Their efforts were extraordinary, and their reach and impact were proving to be unprecedented. They were using both traditional and contemporary forms of outreach, including word of mouth, the Internet, social media, and parties—anything and everything to get the word out. They were hitting up hard their churches, sororities and fraternities, and other social and professional organizations. Former and current colleagues, and friends were hosting drives in their workplaces and at schools. Even elected officials, including then Public Advocate Bill de Blasio, were doing donor outreach and registration on my behalf.

Our mantra was: "Wherever a slew of people, especially African Americans, could be found, so could a member of the 'Save Jen Austin' team."

Shawn was commander-in-chief of a mighty army of soldiers, all determined to find me a match and help me win this war. Lesley was general of the Midwest and the Southeast; Elsa was captain of the New England area; Billy and Theresa were captains of the South; Captain Anne covered Metro New York; Captains Ayo and Kim had New Jersey and satellite stations in California on lockdown; Mom was the nationwide general for the African American church; and there was a contingent of more than one hundred family members, friends, colleagues, and associations acting as lone soldiers. All were organizing, mobilizing, and moving to sign up donors in record numbers.

The mood in our home was serious and tense. We all had responsibilities to keep up. The kids had to stay focused on school and grades. Mommy was putting out all-points bulletins to churches across the nation. I was trying to keep calm and germ-free. And Shawn was holding down the roles of husband, dad and mom, caregiver, case manager, executive, and commander-in-chief of donor drives.

Everybody was on edge. Sometimes we snapped at each other when all we really wanted to show was love—Shawn and me, Mommy and me, Shawn and Mommy, Shawn and the kids, me and the kids, and the kids and Mommy. But there were also moments when the tension was broken with a good laugh, like the night when Shawn was up late planning and mapping drives and pairing them with coordinators. As Shawn sat in our home office glued to the computer, his eyes said it all. He was exhausted. I was up and about, wide awake because I had slept during the day. I had just come up the back stairs of our home and was passing through the office to head down the hall to our bedroom.

As I walked by Shawn, I noticed how worn down he looked, and I exclaimed, "Honey, you look so tired!" Shawn responded immediately, "That's because saving your ass is a full-time job!"

We laughed for days.

The drives were a gift from God. No way to explain it other than to say, "But God." What began as an act of love grew into a movement. Family and friends worked feverishly to find a bone marrow donor for me.

There is no other way to describe the emotions I felt than to use the word "joy." I felt joy in knowing that my search for a donor might help both me and so many others in need. Registrants were informed at the drives that they might not be a match for me, but that they could be a match for someone else. Most pledged that they would go all the way if called upon to help me or someone else. My journey had purpose. My journey was greater than me. My kids would see that this was bigger than me.

What an awesome feeling I had day after day after day hearing of drives and the numbers of people that registered. Several people even said to me through letters, emails, Facebook, calls, and in face-to-face encounters that perhaps it was my God-given purpose to help bring the story of the need for African American donors to the black community. Much like the nurse in the ER when I was quarantined, others also declared that I was chosen by Him, the Almighty, to carry this message. I remember thinking, *What a privilege, what an honor, if this is true. To be chosen by Him—no greater blessing.*

One night as I prepared for bed, I said a prayer of thanksgiving to God for the thousands of people who had come forward to be tested for me and what that likely meant for several other persons also needing a donor. Matches would surely be made for some in need of a transplant. Before ending my prayer, I petitioned God on my own behalf. I selfishly asked that I not be made a martyr, that there be at least one match for me among those who joined the registry. I felt guilty for praying such a selfish prayer, but that's how I felt.

FOURTEEN

Just One Match

On New Year's Day, I started feeling sick. I had a cough I couldn't shake. Three days later, on Monday, January 4, I went to the clinic for a check-up and all seemed okay. But the next day was a completely different story. I felt weak. I could hardly stand.

As soon as Shawn got the kids off to school, he and Mommy took me to New York-Presbyterian's emergency room. Within minutes of arriving, the triage nurse examined me and determined I was dehydrated.

I was placed immediately in a private room in the ER. Soon thereafter, a nurse appeared and advised me that the doctor had ordered an IV with fluids to rehydrate me. The nurse took my right arm and began searching for a vein into which to insert the IV needle, but try as she might, she couldn't fine one. My veins had collapsed. She called for the phlebotomist, who proceeded to jab me with IV needles wherever she thought she might catch a vein—the backs of my hands, my wrists, and in-between my toes. It was excruciatingly painful. And even worse, she couldn't catch a vein either.

Finally, after what must have been at least ten piercing attempts, the phlebotomist caught a vein in my arm and started an IV line.

Chapter Fourteen

Over the next several hours, the ER team pumped several bags of fluid into my body. As the evening hours approached, the attending physician decided to admit me, and then sent me upstairs to the oncology floor to be watched overnight.

Shawn went home to be with the kids when they returned from school. He was acutely sensitive to the fact that just like when I first became ill, they had gone off to school with me at home sick in bed and would be returning to learn I was in the hospital. He wanted to help manage any anxiety they might feel. Mommy stayed with me.

Upstairs on the oncology floor, the medical staff continued pumping me up with fluids. But then, seemingly out of nowhere, my breathing became labored, my chest grew tighter, and I began coughing up blood.

What now? What is going on? I thought. I was hacking up blood and splattering it all over my gown and pillow. My condition had changed from bad to very bad, and now to worse.

Listening to the nurses talking over me, I learned that they didn't have an accurate count of how much fluid I'd been given, but whatever the amount, it was too much. My lungs had been flooded with the fluid, and that was causing me to cough up blood.

Perhaps the count was off because I'd received fluid in the ER first, and then brought upstairs to another department and given more fluid. Whatever the reason, not one of the nurses knew exactly how much fluid I'd been given.

But I knew. The lethargic, drugged up, weak, and in pain patient knew. I tried to jump in and tell them. I'd had no less than four bags in the ER and another three units on their floor.

This is insane! I screamed in my head.

Doctors and nurses began talking over me. To get the fluid off my lungs and help me breathe, I would have to be intubated. I would have to be moved to the ICU to be intubated.

As they went back and forth discussing and debating next steps, my mind began retracing the horrors I went through when intubated at St. Vincent's. I remembered the pain and challenges that came with being intubated all too well. My throat was sore for days. I wasn't able to talk or swallow. I had to learn how to eat again.

I thought, *This can't be happening. Intubated? Not again. All because the nurses didn't have a full count on the IV fluid units.* I understood that those things could happen, even in great hospitals like New York-Presbyterian, but really? Intubated again?

And to add to my angst and fear, I now had to be admitted into the ICU. I'd learned from my first scare at St. Vincent's that being placed in the ICU more often than not signaled a very bad prognosis. Being in the ICU was a sign that I was in a very bad way. Just scared up to this point, now I was petrified.

The attending resident physician came into my room and explained the procedure for intubating me. She proceeded, in a rather matter-of-fact manner, telling me I could die from the procedure, and asking me if I wanted to be resuscitated should I go into cardiac arrest. She then asked for the name of my proxy who would make decisions for me in the event I no longer could. She continued by stating, again in a matter-of-fact tone, that many patients with cancer and other terminal diseases choose not to be resuscitated, but of course the decision was mine.

What am I hearing? Is she telling me I'm going to die? How did I get here? How did this happen? I was fine two days ago, but now I might die tonight. I thought I was doing better. We all believed I would get better. I was going to receive a transplant. I was going to survive cancer. Did this doctor know something no one else had told me?

I became hysterical. I insisted upon talking with Shawn. Mom called him on her cell phone and told him what was going on. Scared enough that I might die, I called out for my kids. I told Mommy to ask Shawn to bring them to the hospital so I could see them one more time. It was 10:00 PM on a school night, but it didn't matter. I needed to see them, kiss them, and tell them I loved them. I needed to say goodbye.

With Shawn on the line, Mom passed her phone to the resident physician who explained that she was simply carrying out her duties and responsibility to inform patients of their rights and options, and that she meant no harm. She told him the procedure was necessary to get the fluid off my lungs. I had to have it. She also said he didn't need to bring the kids. Shawn, in turn, explained to her that my experience of being placed in the ICU and intubated shortly after being diagnosed with leukemia, and later learning I had been given a 99 percent chance of death—coupled with her advising me that I could die from the procedure and asking me if I wanted to be resuscitated if I went into cardiac arrest—was the reason behind what may have seemed to her an overreaction.

I was so panicked that how I physically felt was no longer a thought of mine. I'm sure my breathing was still labored and that I was coughing up blood, but that wasn't my concern. Seeing my kids was all that mattered.

Shortly after 11:00 PM, Kennedy and Channing arrived with Shawn. Although we were in a different hospital, the scene was all too familiar to them. Just as they had witnessed at St. Vincent's three months before, I was laid up in a hospital bed and connected to all kinds of machines with lights, bells, and whistles.

Channing asked my mom, "Are we here to say goodbye to Mommy like last time?" He was just eight years old.

I hugged them and told them I loved them and was proud of them. Shawn kissed me and told me I would be fine. He was so certain of it that he and the kids didn't stay long. He told the kids to give me another hug, and then he took them home.

Hours later I woke up with a tube down my throat and a catheter between my legs—wired up and immobile. *How did this happen?* I was in bad shape again. Really bad shape. Once again, I couldn't talk.

Dr. Roboz came to see me in the ICU and told me that the cold and cough I had a few days earlier had turned into bronchitis, and my body was too weak to fight it. Shawn had told her about the resident attendant's statements to me, and she was both apologetic and sympathetic. She said I had to be informed of what could happen while being intubated, but that she understood why I wished the attending physician had handled the conversation differently. She reassured me I wasn't near death and told me that if ever it came to me being near death, she would let me know. I wouldn't have to learn from a resident.

Dr. Roboz then delivered some unexpected, but encouraging, news. She told me that the donor search had turned up two potential unrelated adult donor matches and four possible cord bloods.

I'm not sure how I responded but I remember how I felt. Hopeful and scared. The potential for a cure? This is what we had been praying for. We knew God could do it, but that didn't mean it would happen. *Oh my God! Oh my God!* But what if the potential adult matches didn't turn out to be viable matches? What if the potential donors were contacted but didn't respond? What if further testing revealed that they really weren't good matches? What if something happened that made the matches unworkable? What if? There were only two of them. What if?

And the cord blood? Really? Cord blood? The treatment alternative was still so new. We hadn't thought much about it because it was talked about as though it was an "only if there isn't anything better" option.

We knew that a cord blood transplant was a growing alternative to an unrelated bone marrow donor transplant, especially for people of color with ethnically diverse backgrounds for whom it is most difficult to find an adult donor. Essentially, stem cells in the umbilical cord blood and placenta that most often are thrown in the trash right after a baby is born are extracted and infused into the patient's body to generate and promote the development of a new blood and bone marrow system. That's right—every time a baby is born there is the potential to cure someone of a blood cancer or other life-threatening blood disorders.

We were so excited, yet nervous. How excited could I allow myself to feel? What if we told everyone that we had a match and it proved unviable? What if everyone stopped looking for a match and it turned out I didn't have one?

But then again, all I needed was one match. If God had one for me, it was just for me. For no one but me.

Shawn and I decided to tell no one until further testing was done.

After a few more days in the hospital, I got better and was released. Still traumatized by the whole incident, I wanted to put it behind me and move forward.

CHAPTER
FIFTEEN

Always

In mid-January I returned to the clinic for a check-up with Dr. Roboz. Mommy came with me. Throughout the visit, I worked hard at keeping the conversation about possible donors and cord bloods to a minimum. Nothing was certain at this point, and so I'd said very little about possible matches to Mom. I didn't want to get her hopes up too high. I tried to talk with Dr. Roboz only about what we were doing in the clinic that day, but I wasn't too successful. Dr. Roboz needed to update me on the search results and next steps, and she had no reason to think Mom wouldn't know about the registered donors and cord bloods that had been identified. She'd been present for so many of my visits where Dr. Roboz and I openly talked. Why would a conversation about good news be any different?

Dr. Roboz performed another biopsy to test for the presence of cancer in my bones. Any signs of cancer would delay and possibly rule out transplant. If the cancer was active at the time of transplant, it would likely corrupt the transplanted bone marrow cells.

Every time I had a biopsy, I spent the next six or seven days that followed holding my breath until the results came back. I was extremely fortunate. Other than the first biopsy, the results came back negative for cancer every time. But God!

After completing the biopsy, Dr. Roboz sat with Mom and me, and advised me that the transplant team had done more work to determine if the identified cord bloods and the unrelated donors were, in fact, real possibilities. They had concluded that the cord blood was the best option. Frankly, it may have been the only real option because 50 percent of registered bone marrow donors never follow through. That number doesn't even include those people who do make themselves available and are tested but then are determined not to be good matches.

I really didn't know that much about the odds related to a transplant. I'd stopped asking questions a long time ago, which was so unlike me. When I first met Dr. Roboz, she advised me to try to avoid managing my medical case, and instead, focus on living. I complied with her request almost to a fault.

I had stopped trying to manage most things—my illness, my home, the drives . . . everything but my feelings and emotions, and my kids. I wanted to be free to truly feel what I was feeling, whatever that was, and to be able to experience it to its fullest. Fortunately, what that translated into was feeling free to live my reality—the possibility of death at a relatively young age, of leaving my children, my husband, mother, brother and sisters, and friends. I had the freedom to be awake in the moment, and to go with it— whatever it was—because I did not know how long I had. I got to live more freely in my reality.

And with this freedom came the gift of clarity. Shawn and I talked about life without me. I'd tell him no girlfriends or marriage for him until Channing graduated high school. Still not sure how sincere a conversation that was on both our parts. I told him that my pictures should stay up around the house for as long as the kids lived with him. Perhaps he should sell the house, but wait at least one year following my death so the kids wouldn't have too much change at once.

We talked about being careful who Shawn allowed to step in to help raise Kennedy and Channing. I warned him that while all of our friends and family are good people, seemingly minor differences in values and beliefs could have a huge impact on our impressionable children.

I got to see my husband for the amazing father he truly is. Our children were facing the very real possibility of my death and having to move forward in life with just one parent. And as scary as that thought was, it was only because I wanted to go on being their mother. The reality was that Shawn Austin would do his best and his best would be good enough. It would be better than good enough.

I'll always remember the time Shawn was on the phone with my cousin LaMarr while sitting in my hospital room with his laptop open doing work. From the moment LaMarr learned I was ill, he unselfishly and selflessly stepped up, alongside Robin and Leigh, to help Shawn with Channing and Kennedy. LaMarr even moved in to be a constant presence and support. He made our kids a primary concern.

Shawn was on the phone with LaMarr coordinating a playdate for Channing and making sure Kennedy had what she needed for a school project. I remember thinking, *If I die, Shawn's going to raise these kids just as we would have together.* I remember thanking God for giving me the gift of clarity to see and appreciate my husband as the best father imaginable for our children.

Clarity also allowed us to talk openly with the kids. I would tell them both that if God took me sooner than we hoped and prayed, they had to accept that because it was my time. I firmly believed and still believe that God gives us life to fulfill his purposes, and that when we have fulfilled them, and not a second before or after, He calls us home.

I would tell them this repeatedly, so much that they began incorporating it into their prayers. Channing would say at dinnertime, ". . . and dear Lord, please make Mommy well, but if you take her we know it's because she fulfilled her purpose."

I had a desire to write more. I became fearful that if I died someone would tell my story for me, and it wouldn't be mine. It wasn't that I believed my family and friends would willfully manipulate my story, but rather that they would bring their own thoughts, feelings, and emotions into their recounting. They would make their stories mine without intending to do so. My experience would become the parable of loved ones who watched and interpreted my thoughts and emotions through their own. If they felt hurt and scared, then of course I did as well. I would hear them on the phone or when people came to visit describing how I was doing and how I felt, and often what I was listening to was their expressions of how they felt.

I understood they were just trying to take care of and protect me, but sometimes it drove me crazy. No one asked me how I was feeling deep down inside, not even my family. What did they truly know about how I felt if we didn't talk about it? Nevertheless, they answered and spoke for me as though they knew exactly what I was feeling. And often they would tell it wrong. All wrong. It made me angry sometimes.

And so I started writing whenever I felt the need. I'd stop anywhere at any time and jot down my thoughts in my BlackBerry.

I Want to Live

I want to live. Lord knows I want to live.

I'm in remission from leukemia but I've been told by my doctors that my chances of long-term survival are small without a transplant.

Even with transplant, I'm still at risk.

Being a child of God, I know that it is He who ultimately decides how long I have on this earth, and that gives me peace.

I trust and I have faith that because of Him, all will be fine.

I told God how I felt:

Sad

Not angry

Not bitter

Not curious at all as to why

Just sad

Being a mother of two young children, I raised with God the question I asked myself over and over:

How Much Longer Would be Enough?

How much longer would be enough?

Enough time to see my daughter grow to her full height and shoe size?

Enough time to see my son's shoulders broaden and his voice deepen?

Enough time to see him walk under the arch from elementary to middle to high school?

Enough time to see them each graduate high school, college, and graduate school?

Enough time to see her find herself and all her glory?

Enough time to see him become the man within him, both strong and sensitive?

Enough time to see them fall in love?

Enough time to help them deal with the hurt that comes with falling in love?

Enough time to see for myself that they're going to be okay?

I Hope They Remember

I want them to remember I wasn't the perfect mom, but I tried real hard.

That I believed in them and tried to give them the opportunities that would help them believe in themselves.

And that I tried to make happy memories that would last and outshine the sad ones.

I hope that when my time comes, they remember how much I loved them and tried to show them, and that will make them smile.

It didn't matter where I was. When the urge to write came over me, I stopped everything.

I remember being in Target one January morning, shopping weeks in advance for Valentine's Day cards for Shawn, the kids, and Mom. As I searched for the right one for Shawn, I began crying. It hit me hard that I'd been focused on doing all I could to prepare my children for a life without me—talking to them, writing them letters, cataloging and tagging personal effects for each of them, and discussing with Shawn their future without me—but I hadn't focused on Shawn living without me. I hadn't written him notes, or talked seriously with him about his life without me. In that moment, right in the middle of Target, the possibility of leaving Shawn hit me hard—really hard. I wasn't ready to say goodbye to him. I pulled out my BlackBerry and I wrote:

Always

As I shopped for Valentine's Day cards for the kids and you, I realized that as I live in two worlds—one full of hope, faith, and belief that God will bring us through, and the other world marked by little acts of preparation in case He has another plan—I so often speak about what I desire for our children, and little about what I desire for you. I thought about this, and soon realized that whereas I do this in part because of who you are—strong, steady, able, and ready whatever the situation—I also do this because I can't bring myself to a place of preparing, if need be, to say goodbye to you. For some reason, I can pull myself together and make plans and preparations for our children, but I can't do this for us. I guess I just think of us as always.

So, if it's "always," know that I've always loved you and I always will, that I've always believed in you and I always will, that I've always admired and depended upon your strength and resolve, and knowing what you're made of increases my comfort that all will be all right. Know that I tried to make you happy, and that I want you to be happy. And finally, know that the selfish person in me hopes that you'll always love me even if I'm not here.

Despite being told about the possibility of two donors or a cord blood transplant, we continued holding drives. We were on a mission. Friends and family, colleagues and church community—all were on a mission. They organized drives, and I engaged national organizations with large numbers of African Americans to encourage them to use my name and story for donor recruitment in cities across the country. Together, we were raising awareness about the need for African American donors. Together, in just thirteen weeks, we added more than 13,000 people to the registry, with the great majority being people who identify as black. We later learned that this was the largest number ever added in connection with one patient's effort and the largest number of African Americans added in one year.

Phone calls, get well cards, and emails poured in from family, friends, friends of friends, and colleagues near and far. I received Facebook messages and friend requests daily from strangers who had heard about my situation and had registered to be a potential match. Meals, fruits, and chocolates from Jack and Jill moms, Berkeley Carroll parents, my sister-friends, church members, and neighbors came in amounts much greater than we could humanly eat and store. Fresh flowers and books decorated our tables weekly. Prayer calls for me were constant and my name was placed on prayer lists in churches around the country. All were tangible reminders that my family and I weren't journeying alone. All were a source of comfort and hope.

CHAPTER
SIXTEEN

Send Me a Sign

Cord blood! Stem cells? Science and modern medicine in the making? Wow! Really?

Dr. Roboz explained to me that cord blood is a risky procedure and that success would not come easy. She explained that the process of cord blood transplant and recovery is most often lengthier and more challenging than bone marrow transplant because the cord blood recipient has no immune system. Right before transplant, the cord blood transplant recipient's immune system is completely wiped out. The same occurs in the case of bone marrow transplant but in that case, the transplant recipient inherits the donor's immune system. With a cord blood transplant, the stem cells are those of a baby, and babies do not have fully-developed immune systems at birth. Cord blood transplantees have to develop new immune systems, rendering them more susceptible to germs and disease at an alarming rate and for an extended length of time.

It all sounded very scary. A transplant wouldn't be a slam dunk at all. In fact, I could die from transplant. But it also sounded like I really didn't have a choice. Transplant was the best and only chance I had at surviving the disease.

Dr. Roboz went on. She invited me to talk with the cord blood transplant physician at Memorial Sloan Kettering Cancer Center before deciding upon where to have the transplant procedure performed. Even though New York-Presbyterian Weill Cornell Medical Center performed cord blood transplants, Dr. Roboz wanted me to meet Dr. Juliet Barker, the cord blood specialist at Memorial Sloan Kettering Cancer Center. Trained at the University of Minnesota where the first cord blood transplant in the world to cure leukemia was performed, Dr. Barker had come to Memorial Sloan Kettering and helped establish the cancer center's cord blood transplant program.

Dr. Roboz surprised me with her suggestion. When we first met, she counseled me to follow her lead and I complied. I had essentially turned the work of managing my case over to her. Now, she was advising me to manage the very big next step—where I would undergo transplant.

Somewhat at a loss, I simply asked Dr. Roboz, "Why would I go to MSKCC?" I wanted Dr. Roboz to tell me what to do. Her response reflected both her brilliance and her integrity:

"Dr. Barker has had great results with several cord blood patients, particularly persons of color with complicated cases. She's straightforward." She continued, "The difference between being transplanted here at New York-Presbyterian and at Memorial Sloan Kettering is like shopping at Bergdorf's versus Saks Fifth Avenue. Same product but different customer service. It's a matter of preference." A few years later when I joined the Board of the National Marrow Donor Program, I learned that several hospitals have greater experience with cord blood transplant, and Memorial Sloan Kettering Cancer Center is one of them.

With my consent, Dr. Roboz immediately set up an appointment for me with Dr. Barker for the very next week. Shawn and I didn't tell anyone. What if upon further review the cords weren't good matches? What if someone else got to them before we did and they were no longer available? What if the cancer returned and they couldn't transplant me? What if I just wasn't a good candidate?

⌒

Shawn and I met with Dr. Barker in late January. When we arrived at Memorial Sloan Kettering Cancer Center, we were directed to the bone marrow transplant suite where I was instructed to fill out what felt like a tomb of forms.

As I poured my four-month medical history out on paper, I stole glances at other patients in the suite, along with their family members and friends. It was easy to tell most of the transplant patients from their caregivers. Just about all of the patients who had already been transplanted had on latex gloves and masks to protect them from the germs of others, and most of them were painfully frail and thin. They looked weak, weary, and worn. Some were in wheelchairs, others walked awkwardly slow. Just about all were draped from their necks to their ankles in blankets. All were in some stage of baldness. And their friends and family, for the most part, looked incredibly supportive and patient.

It was a daunting scene, and yet it was comforting. Everywhere I looked I saw hope. I saw promise. I saw potential. I could be like these patients. I, too, could be transplanted and be sitting here frail and bald, and looking anxious to get cancer behind me and to get on with life.

I was called into the examination room where I met the resident physician. She asked a lot of questions and didn't smile much. She was very matter-of-fact. I didn't feel the warmth to which I had grown accustomed at New York-Presbyterian. I wasn't liking her or Memorial Sloan Kettering.

About a half hour later, Dr. Barker entered the room. She wasted no time. She shook my hand and Shawn's hand and began laying out the plan. She would have her staff do their own cord blood search to ensure the best matches possible were identified. She would order pre-transplant tests of several types for me, including an MRI, a stress EKG to assess the strength of my heart, and pulmonary function testing to examine the cavity on my lung and the overall strength of my lungs.

She directed me to have a dental checkup to ensure I didn't have major dental issues that would affect the transplant. She would also order a psychological review to get a read on whether I would be able to endure the emotional rollercoaster that comes with a transplant. Lastly, she would perform another biopsy that day to make sure there were no signs of cancer. If present, the cancer signs would, at a minimum, delay the transplant to allow time for another round of chemo, or at worst, rule out my chances for transplant.

Dr. Barker then talked about the potential side effects of transplant. Months without an immune system would require being confined in a hospital room for at least five weeks during transplant with limitations on visiting and limited contact with people once at home. Possibly, the transplant could permanently damage or compromise certain organs—my heart, kidneys, and liver.

Dr. Barker began talking about dates for transplant. She threw out dates in mid-February. She said we had to move fast, as quickly as possible.

A few minutes later, our meeting came to an end and Shawn and I walked out of Memorial Sloan Kettering Cancer Center. At first, we were afraid to speak to one another. It was as though we couldn't talk because then we'd no longer be dreaming. But then simultaneously, we realized we both couldn't be dreaming. We were awake. This was real. All signs were pointing toward the very real possibility of a transplant. A life-saving treatment seemed within reach.

But we also recognized that it was not yet time to celebrate, to pick up the phone and shout victory to our friends and family. What if Dr. Barker didn't draw the same conclusions about the cord blood that had already been identified? What if the cord blood units had already been claimed by some other patient? What if I couldn't pass those physical exams? What if the biopsy showed the cancer was back? What if I didn't make it to mid-February? We weren't ready to celebrate.

We told no one.

For the next few weeks, we quietly went about the business of preparing for the possibility of a transplant. I traveled to Memorial Sloan Kettering Cancer Center just about every other day.

Just as St. Vincent's had been a critical part of my earlier journey, the same was now becoming true of New York-Presbyterian. Both hospitals had played substantial roles in delivering me to a point in my journey where I was in remission and being tested for a transplant. Just as when I met Dr. Roboz and never returned to St. Vincent's, once I met Dr. Barker, I never returned to New York-Presbyterian.

I underwent a series of tests and consultations, each one rattling every nerve in my body.

Being trapped in an MRI chamber for thirty minutes with nothing but my thoughts and anxiety.

Walking on a treadmill and fearing I wouldn't be able to go as long as necessary to show my heart was strong enough to endure transplant.

Sitting in a chamber and breathing into tubes to determine the strength of my lungs.

Having another endoscopy to study the cavity in my lungs.

The emotional stress of these tests was overwhelming. Transplant was within reach but there were so many factors, each of which could derail my hopes and dreams. The first days of my journey with cancer had already taught me that nothing is certain. It didn't matter that with each physical test I passed, I was one step closer to transplant. Anything could happen.

I was a bundle of nerves, and poor Shawn had to help manage all of my anxiety by himself. He was my pillow, catching all of my tears and hearing all of my fears.

One morning it all was just too much. As I sat in a patient suite at Memorial Sloan Kettering, waiting for another round of tests, I began thinking, *How did I get here? How is it that my body may not be strong enough? I've always been strong. I was the fit one.* I began to sob. Big tears. I couldn't hold it together. I had survived the first battle. I'd hung on as we searched for a donor. I now had a transplant option. But still, I might not make it. I was facing the very real possibility of an early death.

And then, just as quickly as I was overcome with grief, all sadness disappeared. My soul began crying out, *Hallelujah! Hallelujah! He abides within!*

Filled with excitement, I rummaged through my pocketbook, searching for my BlackBerry. Upon finding it, I pulled it out and typed an email to my siblings. It read:

While I don't wish you any harm, suffering, or despair, I do pray that at some point in your life you get to walk a darksome path with Jesus, and that you're awake in the moment. It's got to be the most amazing journey!

Just like the lyrics of the gospel song by Keith Hunter, "God is Still Moving," God was moving. "I could feel Him in my soul . . . moving in me."

As I progressed from test to test, passing each one, I moved closer and closer to a transplant and closer to God. I found myself having conversations with Him on a variety of subjects that at times felt dichotomous. Conversations about my absolute trust in Him, and yet about my fears of not returning home after the transplant.

Chapter Sixteen

Conversations about holding and walking in two truths—my quest to live, and my desire to prepare my family for a world without me. Conversations about my believing He would give me complete healing, yet seeking to accept that He may have a different plan and my desire to be at peace with that.

I also spent a lot of time debating with myself whether transplant was His plan for me. Was my healing really going to come, in part, from cord blood transplant?

I wanted to know that transplant was well with Him, that I wasn't violating any moral code by employing modern medicine to mess with the natural order of things to extend my life. I needed a sign that God was all right with the way things were going.

One day while on my way to the hospital to have tests run in preparation for the transplant, God provided me just the sign I needed.

As I was walking up the street heading to the hospital, I was talking with God and praying specifically that the transplant would be well with Him. As I approached the street corner, I was stopped by a red light. As I waited for the light to turn green, I was drawn to a woman with a big, blue bag standing on the opposite corner, waiting for the same light to turn green so she could cross and head in the direction where I stood.

For some reason, I became fixated on the woman's bag and I began obsessing about its size and shape, and what it might hold. What was in it? Was it a messenger bag? Was it a dog carrier?

The light turned green, and as I crossed the street, the woman with the bag did the same. Soon we were passing each other, and I got right up on that bag. I quickly saw that it had words written in big, bold letters right on its front:

"National Marrow Donor Program"

Yes, National Marrow Donor Program, the name of the nationwide organization that recruits bone marrow and cord blood donors. The organization that had been helping me.

Here I was on the street in the midst of praying for a sign the Lord knew I desperately needed, and He provided it in that very moment.

I shouted in my head, *Hallelujah!* That was just what I needed to believe all was well with Him, that I would receive this transplant, and that I would be victorious in His name!

A few days later, the call we'd hoped and prayed for came. All tests were complete and the results had been studied. The cords were the best matches, and I'd passed all of my tests. Only one more matter had to be addressed—my mental health. Was I psychologically able to withstand the emotional rigors of the transplant?

My caregivers and I were instructed to come to the hospital to meet with the transplant social worker. Because Mom was also my primary caregiver, she had to come too. Shawn and I had to bring her into the cone of silence.

We decided to tell Mom that the cords Dr. Roboz had talked about during my visit back in mid-January had actually been confirmed and tagged for me, but nothing was definite just yet.

We said nothing about the tests I'd passed. We said nothing about a projected transplant date. I wouldn't be able to stand it if we let her in on everything and got her hopes up only for them to be crushed if the doctors put a stop to the transplant. We were so cautious about what we shared with her that I can't even remember her reaction. I think we downplayed the news so much it seemed to her that transplant was possible but still a long shot at best.

When Mom, Shawn, and I met with the social worker, she had several questions, mostly about my support system. Would anyone be able to stay with me in the hospital during my transplant stay, which would likely be as many as forty days? Would there be someone at home with me at all times during my recovery? Was I a person of faith, and if so, how strong was my faith? Was I emotionally strong? What examples could I provide? And what about my children? Were they okay?

I'll admit I gave answers I thought would help me pass the test. I said what I felt I needed to say to be deemed mentally ready for the transplant. I didn't really answer authentically. I wasn't going to let any emotional stresses prevent me from being transplanted.

I passed this test, too.

In early February, Shawn and I returned to Memorial Sloan Kettering and met again with Dr. Barker. Our meeting was brief. Dr. Barker told me I would be admitted on Wednesday, February 17, and receive the transplant one week later on Wednesday, February 24. She said that date would become my new birthday—the first day of my new life. I smiled. February 24 was my Daddy's birthday, and now it would be mine as well. God was moving, and having fun too.

CHAPTER
SEVENTEEN

Preparing for Transplant

We left the hospital filled with excitement and hope. As we made our way home, we vowed not to tell anyone until just before I entered the hospital.

I spent the next several days preparing for the transplant and for death. When reading about the transplant process and what I should expect, I learned more about the risks associated with transplants. Apparently, as many as 50 percent do not make it through transplants.

So, I got my house in order. I updated my will. I planned for the distribution of my most personal effects, paying special attention to items I wanted Kennedy and Channing to be given at milestone moments in their lives. I labeled the boxes containing the letters I'd written each of them: "On your 13th birthday." I tagged my Women's Bible for Kennedy and my father's Bible for Channing with the words: "As you enter college." There were special pieces of jewelry that I divided between them. Channing would receive my engagement ring, and Kennedy would have my anniversary band.

I went through photo albums, slowly turning the pages of pictures filled with smiles and laughter that memorialized the special times and bonds I'd shared with friends and family. Some images were too precious to keep tucked away in albums should I die, and so I pulled them out and placed them in envelopes with notes to those captured in them. The notes were short and sweet. Most just read, "Love You!" I made sure to mail them before I went into the hospital to be transplanted.

I worked more on my story, the writings that conveyed in my own words my emotions about my illness and my life's journey. I finished my love letters to Shawn.

I repeatedly thanked God and praised Him for the life I'd lived, the family I'd been privileged to have, and the joy I'd known.

I Couldn't Have Loved You More

If things don't turn out the way we hoped, prayed, and planned,

Know that I couldn't have loved you more.

I couldn't have been loved more.

It was a blessing to have received my flowers while living.

I got to witness and experience the power of love and giving.

My life felt complete.

I thank God for my journey.

Every step of it.

He gives us no more than we can bear,

And He watches over His children.

More time would have joyfully increased my testimony.

It wasn't my desire, but it is well with my soul.

Please be kind to my husband, my children, and my mother, my sisters, and my brother.

And my nieces and nephews, and friends.

For they all have been so good to me.

I had prepared for death as best I could. No more worries about whether I could have done more. I'd done the best I could. Channing was clear: if Mommy dies, it's because she has fulfilled God's purpose and it is time for her to go home to be with Him. Kennedy too. They both knew what I expected of them. Their response to my daily question, "If I should die, what do you do?" was firm. Without hesitating they would answer, "I keep going."

Thinking and talking about dying and leaving my children hurt like hell, but we had to do it. I wasn't going to die without trying to give them some coping tools and an understanding that their lives—their futures—didn't end with mine.

Once I felt confident I'd done all I could to prepare for death— as I had prepared my children—I felt free to fight. I turned my attention to the fight ahead of me: surviving the transplant.

The next weekend was President's Day weekend, a three-day weekend. We took the kids to the Berkshires to ski, just as we'd done every year since Kennedy was four. Throughout this ordeal, as much as we could, we tried to live like we always had. Mom came with us. We stayed in the Jiminy Peak townhouses, which were fully equipped with two bedrooms, two bathrooms, a living room, and an eat-in kitchen. Shawn and the kids skied, and Mom and I stayed inside, resting and watching movies.

That Sunday was Valentine's Day. Shawn presented each of us with a box of chocolates. I had my cards for everyone. He and I also had a special announcement. As Mommy and the kids munched on chocolate, I shared that I would enter the hospital that coming Wednesday to receive a transplant one week later.

Joy. Unspeakable joy.

The kids were giddy. Mom was overwhelmed with gratitude. We all donned the biggest smiles as we ate our chocolates.

Even though the transplant was just days away, Shawn and I decided not to share the news with everyone just yet. We knew all too well that anything could happen, and that my transplant could be delayed or derailed. No need to tell the world just yet.

We told no one. Well, Shawn told no one. I told Billy, Elsa, and Lesley, and my sister-friends Anne, Ayo, Bernie, Kim, Theresa, and maybe one or two others.

I moved through those last days before the transplant excited and anxious. Wednesday was both too far off and yet just hours away. I wanted to get on with the transplant, but I was also fearful that I might not make it back home, that I would die and never see my kids again.

And then Wednesday morning came. Everyone showered and dressed. Traveling by car, we all headed out together. We dropped Kennedy off first and then Channing. When they each got out of the car in front of their school buildings, I got out too. I hugged them each as if we were hugging for the last time.

Shawn and I moved through the streets of Brooklyn to the Battery Tunnel on our way to Manhattan. As Shawn drove, I sat in the passenger seat and looked out the window, trying to take in as much as possible. I was clear. I understood that I was potentially looking at the outside world for the very last time.

As we entered the tunnel, my BlackBerry rang. Thinking it had to be one of my siblings, I quickly pulled the phone out of my purse. To my surprise, it was neither of them. It was my friend, Dennis Walcott, the City's School Chancellor at the time, calling to wish me well. I didn't remember telling Dennis I would be admitted for transplant that morning, but I guess I told him, too.

Dennis wished me a good morning. He said he would be thinking of me, and that he knew I would be fine. He then told me to hold on because there was someone else who wanted to speak with me. The next voice I heard belonged to his honor, Mayor Bloomberg.

Mayor Bloomberg said something along the lines of: "Good morning, Jennifer! Just want to wish you a successful transplant." I responded with gratitude. I told him that because of the stem cell research he supported at Johns Hopkins Bloomberg School of Health, I would be receiving a cord blood transplant. He humbly agreed. We chatted a little more, and then hung up the phone. A wonderful surprise and thoughtful gesture indeed.

Shawn and I arrived at Memorial Sloan Kettering Cancer Center at 9:00 AM and headed straight to the surgical prep floor as we had been instructed. First things first, I needed to have a new port placed in my chest because I would receive treatments— pre-transplant chemotherapy, blood transfusions, platelets, the transplant itself, and post-transplant treatments—via the port for the next several months.

Shawn helped me disrobe and prepare for the procedure. We chatted, but not about anything material. We mostly made small talk and giggled. Our excitement and nerves wouldn't allow much more.

At some point that morning, I was transported down to the operating floor where the procedure would take place. Shawn was with me right up until the patient escort placed me in a wheelchair and wheeled me into the operating room.

I woke up later that afternoon in my new home, the hospital room I would live in twenty-four hours a day for the next five weeks or so. It was a tiny room, much smaller than the rooms I'd been told to expect. There was no daybed for a family member to sleep on as I had been told. There was no room to walk around, which I had been informed would be important for my conditioning both pre-transplant and during the transplant hospitalization period. Mommy was there sitting in a chair that was so close to my bed, she couldn't have been any nearer had she been in bed with me.

I didn't complain. Nothing to complain about. I was right where I wanted to be.

I was hungry so Mom picked up the menu on the nightstand and read it to me. Food was served a la carte and room service style. You only ate if you ordered something, and you only ordered what your doctor had previously approved from the menu, which in my case was, once again, a neutropenic diet. Surprisingly, the choices looked pretty good. I ordered a crab cake, tilapia, mashed potatoes, and peas.

When the food arrived, I sat up in my hospital bed to eat. That's when I felt it. That's when the new port made its presence known. Oh, the pain! It was horrendous. Not as excruciating as the pain and trauma I felt months before when the nurse ripped the gauze out of the hole in my chest, but still, it was bad.

Mom pressed the "Call Nurse" button on the remote control hanging from the bed. The remote control had several functions. It controlled the bed settings, the lights in the room, and the television. The nurse came in right away. Upon learning what was the matter, she left and returned quickly with painkillers. I swallowed them up, and within minutes all pain was gone.

The next day I was moved out of that room and into a larger room—one with a big bathroom, a daybed, and space to walk. I hadn't complained but my doctor did. She wanted me in a bigger room because I was going to be living in it round-the-clock for at least five weeks if all went well.

⌒

The preparation for the transplant began that day with my first IV dose of a hybrid chemotherapy cocktail. The cocktail was a combination of high and low chemotherapies designed to wipe out any cancer that lay dormant. Because of the trauma and stress my body had already endured—three rounds of chemotherapy, two intubations, and an unexplainable lung cavity—Dr. Barker didn't want to take any greater risks than necessary, thus the hybrid cocktail.

Dr. Barker had been working on this cocktail as part of a clinical trial. I would be one of the first patients to experience it. I didn't ask to be part of the clinical trial, but felt I had no choice. Dr. Barker thought it was the best chemotherapy pre-transplant regimen for me. I trusted Dr. Roboz, and she trusted Dr. Barker enough to suggest her as my transplant physician, so I trusted her too.

After five days of chemotherapy, I had radiation. Full body radiation. Twice. Twenty minutes each time over two days. A hospital escort met me in my room with a wheelchair. He covered me with a yellow robe, a mask, and blankets, and wheeled me to the elevators and down to the radiology floor. Then he turned me over to the radiation technician who administered the radiation as the doctor had prescribed.

The technician was a black man, probably in his mid-to-late fifties. He wore dark glasses and skinny jeans. He said little, but he sang Michael Jackson songs the whole time I was with him. He told me to stand against a board the full length of my body. Once I did, he strapped me in from head to toe. He told me to bend my legs slightly, tilt my head forward, and plant my chin on an uncomfortable metal bar. I felt like I was in a guillotine of sorts.

Preparing for Transplant

Feeling awkwardly positioned and restrained, just as the radiation commenced, I began thinking that I couldn't possibly stand like this for a full twenty minutes of treatment.

Then, with just under five minutes of treatment time remaining, I became nauseous. I tried not to think about how I was feeling. I tried to ignore the escalating queasiness, but it didn't work. With less than four minutes of treatment to go, I got sick. I vomited all over myself and the belts that were holding me up.

The technician came to my rescue quickly. He stopped the radiation, unstrapped me, and cleaned me and the straps up. He gave me a few minutes to recover, and then he resumed the radiation and I completed the treatment.

I no longer felt sick, but I was anxious that I might have to start the treatment over. The technician assured me that I wouldn't. I felt relieved.

The next day, the technician and I were both prepared. He had a spit pan on a cart next to the radiation apparatus, and I had a plan. I wasn't going to count down the minutes. I wasn't even going to look at that countdown clock. I was going to just push on through. I did and it worked.

The very next day was February 24—Transplant Day.

My new birth/rebirth day.

CHAPTER
EIGHTEEN

Transplant

I don't remember much about the actual day of my transplant. Perhaps that's because there wasn't much to remember. Shawn was there with me in the room. Lesley and Elsa, too. My nurse brought in the bags containing the cord blood to be infused into my body and presented them to me. They looked like ordinary pints of red blood. She then connected the bags to the IV drip. As the cord blood began to flow through the tubes, Lesley, Elsa, and Shawn stood around me and Shawn prayed. He prayed a prayer of thanksgiving and healing.

I don't remember much else except that I fell asleep, just like I'd done on several other occasions in my life that were just too big for me to handle all at once. I fell asleep while taking a high stakes organic chemistry exam in college. I checked out for twenty-two minutes when taking the New York State Bar. And I slept in a coma for ten days when my body began to shut down from the effects of cancer back in September. Perhaps falling asleep is the way I manage big stress.

In the days that immediately followed transplant, I felt good, or relatively good. I was getting up and out of bed and moving around the room. I did have a few challenges, but nothing that seemed unmanageable.

Chapter Eighteen

I developed a severe case of congestion. It seemed like I had the transplant on Wednesday and woke up Thursday unable to breathe through my nose. One of the attending physicians prescribed a nasal saline, and I snorted it like an addict snorts cocaine, but it didn't really work.

I started bleeding vaginally within a few days of undergoing the transplant. Given that I hadn't had a period since November, I thought that was a good thing. But when I started passing blood clots, I became very concerned. I'd never had blood clots before. I told the doctors immediately and they prescribed estrogen and told me the clotting should subside. It did, but they kept me on estrogen for reasons I wouldn't learn until later.

On lockdown in the room, I was like the boy in a bubble. I couldn't leave the room unless there was an emergency or I needed a medical procedure such as an x-ray or sonogram that couldn't be performed in the room.

On lockdown in a room with a bathroom, a TV, a computer, a daybed, a chair, and space to take five steps, turn around, and take five more.

I had books, lots of books, but I didn't have the attention span to read them. I remember the doctor saying that the chemo and radiation could cause temporary loss of the ability to concentrate. So was the case for me.

Being confined didn't get to me too much because I understood why it was necessary, and I wanted to live. But there were occasions when cabin fever set in, when I longed to be out there—not out of the hospital—just on the other side of the door in the hall, walking around like some of the autologous patients who'd been transplanted with their own stem cells and hadn't had their immune systems wiped out completely.

The first time I had a case of cabin fever, my mind came to my rescue. Almost instantly, I thought of Nelson Mandela and the strength and courage he displayed for the world in enduring imprisonment for twenty-seven years. Drawing inspiration from his incredible journey, I told myself, "If Mandela can survive years in a cell box, I should be ashamed to complain about forty days in a tricked-out hospital room." From that moment forward, I had very few moments of self-pity. Any such thoughts were fleeting.

I do remember being anxious for the transplant results, though. We would know within the first seven days, based on blood tests, if the cords appeared to be taking control of my blood-making system. Within thirty days, we'd have data that would tell us whether the cords had, in fact, taken over.

I kept thinking and praying, *Complete Healing.*

I quickly developed a routine to pass the time each day. I would aim to sleep as long and as late into the morning as I could, but that attempt always proved futile. Between nursing aides weighing me, taking my temperature and blood pressure, and collecting my urine to measure my output every other hour throughout the night, and phlebotomists poking me at 5:00 AM, I never slept long or late. And by 7:00 AM, Shawn or Mom, whoever of the two had stayed with me the night before, would be moving about and getting ready for the day.

Chapter Eighteen

Sometime around 7:30 AM, we would call home so I could talk to the kids before they left the house for school. Most often Mom and Shawn would be on each end of the call—one at the hospital and the other at home. Sometimes LaMarr, Robin, or Leigh would be on one end of the call. They would line-up the plays of the day—who would pick Channing up from school or a playdate, and who would pick Kennedy up from swim team practice, or take her to dance or debate. I listened and sometimes weighed in, but I mostly listened. Shawn was the orchestra leader and everyone else was playing in perfect harmony.

I ordered breakfast by 8:00 AM. It was pretty much the same breakfast every morning: cereal, a hard-boiled egg, and toast.

Shortly after breakfast, a nursing aide would arrive and prep me for a shower. There were three different aides who covered my room, and they all performed the same role: getting me out of bed and moving. The aide was responsible for covering my port with a waterproof bandage to keep water and soap from coming in contact with it and causing possible infection. She gave me towels and lotions to keep my skin from drying out. And while I showered, she stayed just outside of the bathroom in the room proper, changing my bed sheets and listening to make sure I was okay.

As I progressed through transplant, things did become more challenging at times. There were days when I felt too weak, too tired, and too emotionally exhausted to shower. On those days, any one of the aides would push me unmercifully. Not one would cut me any slack. Though annoying, it was necessary, for on those days if I didn't shower I wouldn't have gotten out of bed. Those were the dark days.

Yes, the dark days. The days when transplant was almost too much. The days when my body swelled up with fluids, instantly adding as much as twenty pounds to my frame and making me feel grossly uncomfortable. Days when I passed blood clots so big that it felt like my uterus had dropped out of my body, and I felt certain I was dying right there in the hospital bed, not from cancer or the transplant but from the loss of blood.

Those were the days when I didn't recognize myself. When I looked in the mirror and saw a person with lips and eyelids three times the size of my own. When I saw a bald head and a skin color so unfamiliarly dark. The radiation's side effects had been immediate. The little hair I had grown back on my head from my first round of chemotherapy had fallen out, and the light skin I'd known as my complexion all my life had become darker, much darker. I'd been forewarned about both side effects, but I still had to adjust. Whenever I passed by the mirror in my bathroom, I'd sneak a peek at myself and wonder, *Who is this woman? Who is this person?* It wasn't me.

But it was. Occasionally, I would stand in the bathroom, in front of the mirror, and stare at the face looking back at me. I'd stare until I saw the person I was looking for. Sometimes it took a while, but ultimately, I found her. I always found her. Her eyes and her smile were the same. She was still there. I was still there.

To keep physically active, I took up pole dancing. With one hand holding my iPod and the other holding and steering my IV pole, I moved around the empty space in my room dancing with as much energy as I could to Donnie, and Marvin, and Dwayne, and John, and Yolanda, and Mary, and McFadden, and Will, and many other

169

gospel and R&B artists. I had a good time with myself whenever I could muster up the energy to move my body. Sometimes Shawn would dance with me. Those moments with him were pure joy.

Within the first several days, my count readings came back and the news was good. The cords were taking hold.

With that positive, early sign, I tried to meet every day with optimism. I would anticipate news of good numbers that indicated the cords were taking control, and news that I would be going home soon. I tried to shower and be dressed every day before the doctors and nurse practitioners made their morning rounds, so that when they arrived at my room they saw an image of strength and readiness to get on with the next stage of the transplant.

I also worked hard to be up and moving for my guests—the family members and the many friends from every part of my life who went out of their way to visit with me. I couldn't control my appearance, but I was going to try like hell to control my affect. Elsa, Billy, Lesley, Brian, and Natalia each spent several nights in the hospital, providing me company and Mommy and Shawn much-needed rest. Colleagues and friends took time from their busy schedules to sit with me and talk for hours about things other than me being sick.

I got to see Kennedy about once a week. Shawn or Mom would bring her. She would suit up in her mask and yellow gown, come in my room, say a few words to me, and then find something else to focus on. A television show or book. Something other than me. I was fine with that. Seeing her was enough.

I hated that Channing couldn't come. He was too young to visit. Too young and too many germs. It broke my heart and his, too, that we couldn't visit. I missed him terribly and desperately wanted to see his little round face and springy curls.

However, one day while looking out the one window in my room as I danced with the pole, I realized that I could see the people on the sidewalk across the street from the hospital. Even though I was on the eighth floor, I could actually make out their faces.

When Shawn came to the hospital later that evening, I told him about my discovery. I walked him over to the window and showed him. I pointed in the direction of the corner where earlier that day I had seen people, their eyes and mouths, their hands and their feet. It was dark, though, and we couldn't see people as clearly. Everyone looked like stick figures. But Shawn indulged me as I explained with excitement that he could bring Channing up to the hospital on the weekend and stand with him across the street so we could see each other and wave.

That next Sunday morning around 10:00 AM, Shawn called me on my cell. He told me to walk over to the window and look down at the corner. I did, and within seconds I saw my baby! I could see Channing, his little round face and his curly locks. He waved and jumped up and down. I could see him, but he had a hard time seeing me. Shawn told Channing where to look and counted windows and floors with him. But it was hard. The sun was shining, making it nearly impossible for him to look up and into a window to see me. But he kept trying. Shawn gave him his cell phone and we talked as we each stood in our respective places, eager to see as much as we could of one another. We blew each other heartfelt kisses.

News that I could go home couldn't come fast enough. Sometimes the days were too long and the weeks just dragged on. It was helpful to know that my hospital stay would be approximately forty days, but actually getting through those days as time went on was a pill that proved too big to swallow. I was in my wilderness.

I attempted to focus on the milestones. Eating table food and keeping it down, as opposed to being nourished intravenously, would indicate that I had a good appetite and could physically process food. The more I ate and held on to what I ate, the sooner I'd be able to go home. When I stopped passing blood clots the size of oranges, I'd be closer. Swallowing my anti-rejection horse pills and thirty-something other pills daily instead of receiving the same meds through an IV would signal that I could manage my medicine regimen at home. Once my red counts, white counts, and platelets stabilized and I didn't require daily transfusions, I'd be ready. I was working hard to do all of the above, so every time I slipped back on any one of these indicators, I was devastated.

After three weeks of being cooped up in the room with my counts all over the place, uncontrollable vaginal bleeding I didn't understand, another round of hair loss, excess water weight with swollen lips and eyes and limbs, skin irritations and rashes, severe deconditioning that was making it hard for me to stand and walk at times, liver and kidney complications, daily red blood cell and platelet transfusions, and weeks without being a mommy to my children, I couldn't take it anymore.

Friends called wanting to visit, and I made up excuses about why it wasn't a good day. It wasn't that I didn't want to see anyone or that I didn't want to be seen. I just didn't feel up to entertaining. Every time someone came to see me, I felt like I had to be on, like I had to manage the visit and the conversation. I just wasn't in the mood.

I even stopped taking calls from my siblings. I only talked with Shawn, the kids, and Mommy. I was reaching my breaking point. It was too much. I was tired. I didn't know if I was going to make it. I didn't know how much longer I could fight.

I began to long for rest. Complete rest. Rest from the suffering and the ups and downs. Sweet rest. Eternal rest. I started to daydream about Heaven and what it would be like to be with God and Jesus. I secretly imagined myself in Heaven hanging out with my daddy. I was the youngest in my family, the child who didn't have as many years with Dad here on earth. But in Heaven, I'd have him to myself. No siblings, no Mommy. Just him and me. These thoughts were more than comforting. They were downright exciting. I started preparing for my departure. I was mentally and emotionally shutting down. I began yearning for peace and joy. Rest. I revisited these thoughts over and over.

One day while in the throes of this deepening retreat, Elsa snuck in for a visit. I can't remember any of what we talked about, but I do remember that she quickly understood that I was disconnecting. I was spiraling down. Elsa asked the attending nurse to call for a mental health specialist.

Chapter Eighteen

A psychiatrist soon arrived and proceeded to ask me a series of questions. I have no idea what I answered, but whatever it was I said, my words qualified me for anti-depressants and sleep medication. I elected not to take the anti-depressants, but I did take the sleeping pills.

I fell asleep soon after, while still fantasizing about eternal rest. My fantasizing continued as I slept. I had a dream. But unlike my daydreaming where I had been able to control where my mind wandered and what was happening to me, I had less influence over my dream as I slept. But God did.

The dream began with me being dropped from the sky in a big egg. When the egg reached the ground, it cracked open. Not knowing where I was, I used the cracked opening to look out. All I saw was an empty, expansive field.

Afraid to venture out, I kept peeking through the crack. After peering out a few times, I spotted moving objects in the far-off distance. Something about them seemed familiar. The objects were erect figures moving in unison. They had different forms—some tall, some shorter, some wide, and some narrow. However, they all shared one common characteristic: each figure had something at its highest point.

After a few seconds of deliberating with myself, I sensed there was something very familiar about these figures, something that signaled safety and direction. I climbed out of the egg and hurried toward them. As I got close to them, my intuition was confirmed. I discovered that the figures were ladies wearing hats on their heads.

I then recognized two of them as women from my home church. Ha! The moving objects were church ladies.

I caught up and began walking with them. Just as I did, out of nowhere there appeared a trolley. It was approaching us from behind. Floating in the air, it was reminiscent of a scene in a Harry Potter movie.

I continued walking with the women, surmising that they must have been headed somewhere good and safe, perhaps church. But now the trolley had my attention. I kept walking alongside the ladies but with my head turned toward the trolley.

There were several people seated on the trolley. At first I couldn't make out any of their faces, but then, all of a sudden, I recognized one. It was the face of the only person I longed to see.

To my surprise and delight, my daddy was on that trolley, sitting and talking with someone as if he was on a leisurely bus ride. Maybe he was talking with someone I knew. Could have been my grandfather or grandmother. I was just so excited to see my dad that at that moment, no one else mattered. I started calling to him, "Daddy, Daddy."

He didn't answer.

I started jumping up and down, and waving my hands, and calling again, "Daddy, Daddy."

Still, he didn't answer. He didn't even look my way.

I got angry. I started shouting, "You see me. Look at me." Then suddenly, I woke up.

And immediately I knew.

It's not my time to die.

God wanted me to know it wasn't my time.

In the midst of my suffering, to keep me from giving up the fight, God spoke to me, and He used a most convincing and influential figure in my life to do it. If in my dream my father had acknowledged me, the fight would have been over. No more struggle. If in my dream my father had turned his head ever so slightly toward me, I would have taken his gesture as a sign from God that it was time to let go.

But God knew better. Knowing me best, He sent the one who always acknowledged my presence, the one whose nod and approval I constantly sought, the one whose refusal to even glance at me would remove all doubt that the war was mine to win.

From that moment on, my focus shifted to getting out of the hospital and getting on with life. I regained my desire and my will to fight. I started eating and dancing again, writing emails, and talking on the phone. I put forth the most positive attitude possible. I was getting myself ready to go home to my family and friends, to my life here on earth.

⟜⟝

Just a few more days passed, and finally I heard the news I'd longed for. The doctors told me that there was a good chance I would be released from the hospital and sent home right before Easter.

My remaining days in the hospital were routine. Time passed slowly as it always does when you're eager to move on.

When the word came that my release would be in just a few days, the clock suddenly sped up. Much to do and much to be learned. I had to learn how to protect my port from infection and water. I had to learn how to manage my pill intake. I had over forty pills, which had to be taken at different times. Some at 7:00 AM, some at 8:00 AM, some at 2:00 PM, then some at 7:00 PM and at 8:00 PM, and some more at 10:00 PM. This would continue to be my life: sleep in-between pill intake. At least for the next indefinite while.

I had to be trained on what I could eat and how the food I ate had to be prepared and packaged. No lettuce unless it was thoroughly scrubbed, and no fruits like blueberries or strawberries where the skin is edible but difficult to clean. No foods kept in the refrigerator longer than two days. And no ordering in unless it was a pizza pie that wasn't pre-cut. Just like before when I was out in the real world after I first became ill, I had to avoid the risk of bacteria on any food, as well as on the utensils used to prepare it. Eating out was out of the question.

I had to be trained on how to protect myself from others, including family. At home, only I could use the bathroom in my and Shawn's bedroom. Shawn would have to shower, brush his teeth, and handle his business in another bathroom. I'd have to keep my distance from Kennedy and Channing, my walking germ carriers.

No hugs and kisses. No sex.

When I left the house, I had to wear a mask and gloves to protect me from airborne bugs and germs transmitted through physical contact. Handshaking wasn't advised. Neither were crowds and public places. Minimal contact with people outside of family for at least the first one hundred days following transplant.

The doctors were going to let me out of the hospital, but I had to remember that my immune system was nonexistent and I had to act accordingly. It had been wiped out on purpose to enable the cord bloods to transplant without being rejected. The rebuilding of my immune system was just beginning. Any bacteria, virus, food poisoning, or any other thing that could be just an inconvenience or annoying disruption for someone with a functioning system could have deadly consequences for me.

I had to stick to the rules. Any slip-ups could prove deadly. Literally.

Good Friday came. I was going home. Admitted on Ash Wednesday, in my wilderness about forty days, and out by Easter. That not only sounded good, it sounded right. The parallel to the time Jesus spent in the wilderness being tested didn't escape me. I couldn't have planned the timing any better, and I didn't even need to try. God already had.

CHAPTER
NINETEEN

Post-Transplant

Shawn arrived at 1:00 PM to take me home. He entered my room for the first time wearing no mask or gloves.

The attending nurse handed me a large, brown shopping bag full of medications, and together we reviewed my intake schedule. She also alerted us that an earlier blood test revealed that I had CMV, a common and active virus in many people that comes and goes. She said I still could go home and be treated for the virus as an outpatient.

I was instructed to return to the hospital the coming week on Monday, Wednesday, and Friday for clinic visits. My doctors told me that at least three weekly visits would be required for the first several months. Thereafter, visits would gradually shift to two per week, then one, and then biweekly, followed by monthly, quarterly, and eventually, semi-annual and annual visits.

The message was clear: I was going home but the road ahead was still a long and challenging one.

Shawn and I said goodbye to all of the nurses and aides. Still weak and frail, I was wheeled out of my room to the elevators, down to the first-floor lobby, and out the front door of Memorial

Sloan Kettering Cancer Center to the passenger side of our car. I was on my way home.

The kids were ready for Easter Sunday, all because of my early planning neurosis. I'd gotten their Easter clothes back in February before I'd gone into the hospital for transplant. I'd made arrangements with my friend, Theresa, for Kennedy to go to the hair salon with her and her girls Saturday afternoon. Channing would be fine without a haircut. He was still wearing his hair in curls that cascaded down his back, so he had no need of a haircut. They would look their best for Easter Sunday, as has been the tradition for generations in our home and church.

Shawn made sure we were also ready for our traditional Easter egg hunt. When Kennedy was four years old, we began having an Easter egg hunt at home following Easter dinner. This year would be no different. Shawn made certain of that. He pulled out the pastel and neon colored plastic eggs I had purchased in prior years and the bags of bite-size Snickers, Butterfingers, and mini packets of M&Ms he picked up earlier in the week. Together we stuffed the candy and money in the plastic eggs.

On Easter morning, Shawn, Channing, and Kennedy dressed for church. I couldn't go with them, as I couldn't be in crowds just yet and I couldn't receive the hugs and kisses that people at church would be eager to give me and I'd be as eager to receive. I took the kids' pictures before they left.

Mom stayed home to look after me. I wasn't to be left alone.

Post-Transplant

The first order of business was to shower and get dressed before Shawn and the kids returned from church. Mom helped me prepare to shower. I sat in my bedroom in an armchair as she covered my port just as we had been instructed. Mom then went into the bathroom inside my bedroom—my bathroom—and started running the shower.

I got undressed and began making my way to the shower when the phone rang. I couldn't move fast enough to get to it in time to answer. By the time I reached the phone, the caller was gone but the caller ID number was on the screen. Looking at the caller ID, I knew right away it wasn't a call I wanted to return. The first three digits in the number were all too familiar. Someone from the hospital had called. Why were they calling me?

I begrudgingly returned the call. It was Maria, the nurse practitioner. The doctors were now more concerned about the CMV level that had shown up in my blood. Even though people walk around every day with CMV, they didn't think I should. It was too risky. My body might be too weak to fight the infection if I stayed on the outside. I had to be in the hospital, confined again and treated for ten days. And I had to come back in that day, that afternoon, Easter Sunday. I pleaded for more time. Maria gave me until that evening. I could eat dinner and participate in the Easter egg hunt, but right afterward I had to go back in.

I was devastated. I'd just gotten home. I was with my children. It was Easter. I was moving forward. But no, no I wasn't. I was on my way back to the hospital not even forty-eight hours since coming home.

Chapter Nineteen

Numb. That's what I wanted to feel. Numb. That would be easier.

But instead, I felt much, much more. I was hurting.

When Shawn and the kids returned home, I told them the news. Just as we'd been upfront with the kids from the very beginning when I became ill and the doctors said I wasn't going to make it—when essentially, we had no choice—I thought it best to be upfront and let them know I had to head back to the hospital in a matter of hours. The disappointment registered immediately on everyone's faces. We all were in disbelief. How could this be happening? We thought we were moving forward, closing the hospital chapter of this epic drama. No, not quite. Not yet.

Shawn cooked dinner. He made ribeye steak that was superbly seasoned and cooked to perfection. We sat and ate together with LaMarr and Mommy. Though happy to be together, sadness hovered over the dinner table like a giant cloud. We were still in shock. I kept thinking, *I shouldn't have called back. I should have ignored the call.* But I knew I couldn't. Too much was at risk.

As soon as we finished dinner, Shawn and I went outside to hide the eggs. Though frail and extremely thin, I kept up with Shawn—or perhaps he slowed down for me—and together we placed eggs all around the yard.

When we finished placing the eggs up under bushes, on tree branches, and in the grass and dirt, we sat down on the front porch steps and waited for Channing and Kennedy to come out of the house. Neither of us said a word, but we each knew how the other felt. If getting to transplant was like climbing up the rough side of the mountain, post-transplant recovery was going to be like coming down the other side on our backsides, sometimes sliding and sometimes encountering rocks and bumps every inch of the way.

Shawn called out, "Ready, Set, Go!" and off they went! There were fifty-eight eggs to be found, twenty-nine for each of them. Kennedy and Channing ripped through the yard, looking up in the trees for eggs perched on low hanging branches, underneath prickly bushes for eggs half-buried, and on the lawn furniture for eggs nestled between seat cushions. They jumped in the reflection pool that was drained and found a few in the corners. They ran onto the side porch to collect a few sitting in planters.

For the few minutes it took them to scurry around and grab up all the eggs, life felt normal. We all were happy and carefree.

Kennedy collected twenty-nine eggs, and then joined me on the iron bench in the yard. As she opened her eggs to count her money and examine her candy, I told her I was sad to have to leave them again. Even though I didn't say it, she could see I was also tired and weary. I wanted her to know how I felt so she would feel comfortable expressing her frustration too. I was giving her the green light to go ahead and kick and scream, stomp around, fall out on the floor—to demonstrably express the anger I wanted to but couldn't because I'm the mommy.

But Kennedy didn't. To the contrary, she did something completely unexpected. Seemingly without hesitation, almost as if she'd prepared for this moment, she responded, "Mommy, look at this hospital stay as a bug on your windshield. You're going to get rid of that bug and keep on driving."

Chapter Nineteen

When we arrived at the hospital, I was placed in a small box of a room where I was to be holed up for the next ten days while I received medication intravenously to treat the virus. I was told immediately that I couldn't leave the room to walk the corridors of the floor. It was too dangerous. I might acquire another infection.

I understood but it still didn't make sense. I'd been out in the world for two days, but now I couldn't leave my hospital room. Having breathed the air outside of the room on the transplant floor and on the busy New York City streets, this brief stay was already proving to be more difficult than the actual forty plus days of the transplant process.

I'd come so far. Returning to the hospital so soon after being released and resuming some semblance of everyday family life was a major setback, even if only an emotional one. It was too much.

And it was just the beginning.

Post-transplant hospital stays became routine, although I was never emotionally ready for one. Nate, a cord blood transplant survivor who Lesley met in Cleveland, and who came to see me during my transplant stay, had warned me. When he visited me at Memorial Sloan Kettering in the early days of transplant, he told me about his numerous hospital stays post-transplant. He told me that recovery would be replete with good days and bad days, setbacks, and disappointments. I had listened to Nate, all the while thinking that my transplant recovery would be different. *That won't happen to me,* I had thought. I was going to get through the transplant, go home, and get back to living a normal, hospital-free life.

I was wrong.

Over the six months that followed the transplant, I had more than fifteen stays, most of which were triggered by undetected bacteria on food or graph versus host disease (GVHD) flare-ups when my "host body" made attempts to stamp out the newly grafted stem cells. Because I still was within one hundred days of receiving the transplant, my immune system was pretty much nonexistent, and thus, I was highly susceptible to contracting an illness or suffering from GVHD.

It was awful. I'd be at home getting along just fine, feeling like I was growing stronger with each day that passed. I would elect to go down the stairs from my bedroom on the second floor to eat my meals in the kitchen rather than being served in bed. I would add a block to my neighborhood walks in the afternoon with LaMarr, who worked from home most days so I'd have a caregiver, especially when Mom was working. And just when I began thinking I really might be turning the corner, sickness would take over. I'd grow nauseous and wouldn't be able to keep anything down. I'd vomit and have diarrhea to the point that I became dehydrated almost instantly.

Most of these episodes would occur at night. Shawn would come up from the kitchen and find me slumped over in the bathroom. He would help me up, move me to the bed, and take my temperature. We would hope it was lower than 100.6 degrees because if it was 100.6 or higher, I was required to call the attending physician on duty at Memorial Sloan Kettering. And more likely than not, if it was 100.6 or higher, I would have to go in and stay at the hospital—at least overnight.

Chapter Nineteen

The attending physician always instructed me to come in. We would arrive at the emergency room and I would immediately be placed in isolation in a private room. Everyone around me had to wear masks and gowns to protect me from further harm.

Each time I would wish to be sent home, and each time the attending doctor would keep me overnight. More often than not, the overnight stay would turn into a multiple day stay—sometimes as many as twelve days.

Unpredictability at its finest.

For the most part, I dealt reasonably well with this part of my journey. I'd been forewarned by enough people that it would be months before I'd begin to feel like myself. I did my best to manage the physical limitations and the boundaries, as well as the numerous nighttime runs to the hospital that were so frequent they eventually became almost routine. I came to anticipate the signs and the symptoms that would land and keep me in the hospital, along with the anxiety and frustration I worked hard at managing each time. But I did have my moments. Times when it was just too much.

Mother's Day was such a time. It had been more than six weeks post-transplant, and I was looking forward to being at home with my husband, my children, and my mother to celebrate the day. It was supposed to be extra special. Just months before, none of us— Shawn, the kids, or me—felt certain I'd live to see Mother's Day. Having been transplanted, we had reason to hope that I might even see more Mother's Days, but we weren't sure. We had a lot to celebrate and we had a lot for which to be thankful. But the

Tuesday before, sickness took over. GVHD kicked in, and I had to be hospitalized and placed on steroids for several days. I was crushed. My dreams of spending the day like most families and like we'd done so many times before—at home with my children—were at risk of being shattered.

As the days quickly passed, it became painfully clear that I was not going to be released in time to celebrate Mother's Day at home with my family. The attending physician wasn't going to release me. He hadn't said such, but given all my stays, I knew the drill. It was Friday, I was still hooked up to an IV, and no one had said anything about me going home. Even though it had been determined that I had GVHD in my stomach and a local steroid had been prescribed and administered to treat it, they weren't going to let me out of the hospital just yet. Wasn't happening.

I was devastated. The ups and downs of transplant were getting the best of me. The inability to plan, to look ahead, and to enjoy my family was killing my spirit. I began to let my frustration show. I began to sulk. I became irritable. I didn't want to hear or engage in small talk. I had no use for niceties. I was short with people, especially those closest to me like my mom. She tried her best to keep my spirits up, and I worked just as hard to reject her efforts. I couldn't help it.

Saturday morning, the doctor visited my room and confirmed I wouldn't be released that weekend. But before I could wallow in my disappointment, he gave me permission to have Shawn and both Kennedy and Channing visit me on Mother's Day. Because of hospital guidelines, I wouldn't have even dreamed of Channing visiting, as he had been too young to be on the transplant floor.

But fortunately, for this hospital stay, my room happened to be on another floor with fewer restrictions. As long as Shawn promised that Channing had no signs of sickness and would not linger on the floor outside the room, he could come and stay for a little while—an hour or so.

That Sunday as Mom and I played scrabble on the portable table that extended across my bed, Shawn, Kennedy, and Channing appeared at my hospital room door donning hospital gowns and masks, and carrying a food warmer bag filled with delights they had prepared. My little guy looked adorable in his gown that was way too long, gloves that were way too big, and a mask that kept sliding down below his chin.

We dined on fried chicken, rice, and green beans. It was the best Mother's Day dinner I'd ever had.

Once again, God provided. Being with my family was all I wanted, and more importantly, all I needed to keep pressing on.

CHAPTER
TWENTY

It Ain't Over 'til It's Over

Between hospital stays I had clinic visits. Too many to count. Mom, LaMarr, or Shawn accompanied me. At every visit, my blood was tested to check my red blood cell count, my white blood cell count, and my platelets. They were all over the place from week to week. Some days they were inching up in the right direction, and on many other days, they were sliding backwards. When moving in the wrong direction, I instantly feared the worst. Was my body rejecting the transplant? Had the cancer returned?

My emotions vacillated between joy and fear. I remained in a constant state of awareness that, just as I had come down with cancer without forewarning, my cancer-free status could change at any time. I looked to Dr. Barker for assurance that even with numbers flip-flopping all over the place, I was okay. She would firmly remind me that she'd let me know if and when it was time to worry. I followed her orders but paid no attention to her admonition about worrying. I couldn't. I had post-traumatic stress.

Still do.

Over time, my visits to the doctor lessened. I went from three visits weekly to twice weekly by the summer. Eventually, I graduated to just once weekly clinic visits. Then, biweekly, monthly, bi-monthly, and eventually six-month intervals between visits. Of course, there were weeks where the number of visits was doubled, typically after I had a hospital stay and needed more frequent monitoring.

At each visit, Dr. Barker would adjust my medication. Starting with more than fifteen medications and over forty pills daily, she adjusted my pill intake up and down depending on my counts. She told me there would come a time when I would be just about pill-free. It seemed hard to believe with all the pills I was swallowing daily. But she kept her word. My favorite days were when she'd take me off a certain medication. That didn't happen often, which made the experience all the more gratifying when it did.

Though grateful for every day, I began to live for milestones. Surviving the first one hundred days post-transplant was a big deal, especially because it came with approval to eat out. Wow! I could sit in a restaurant and order more than pizza. I had to ask that the food be served as soon as it was cooked and plated, and not be put under a heat lamp. Sometimes that required more explanation about my illness, but so what? I was used to just about everybody knowing about my sickness.

In due time, instead of counting hospital stays, I began counting the days between hospital stays as they were growing significantly in number.

In June, I began taking my kids to and from summer camps.

In August, we were allowed to travel out of state—no more than two hours. We went to the Poconos. I played miniature golf with Shawn and the kids, ate dinner at a diner, and dipped my toes in the hotel pool.

September 2010 was just like many other Septembers in recent years. Summer vacation was over, the kids were back in school, Shawn was back at work, and soon, after this year-long, epic journey, I would be returning to work. Birthday mania was upon us. Shawn's dad's birthday was just a few days away on the 14th, Shawn's on the 21st, Kennedy's on the 23rd, Mom's on the 28th, Matt's the 30th, and mine on October 1. September would be no different than it had been since Kennedy was born thirteen years earlier—chock full of back to school activities and birthday celebrations.

Then again, it would be different, and excitingly so.

Afterword

Awake in the Moment

One evening, several months after my transplant and after I'd fully resumed the life of a working mother and wife, I attended a revival service in Brooklyn to hear my dear friend and brother, Dr. Claybon Lea, Jr. preach. He had served as an assistant pastor to my father at our home church, Bethany Baptist Church, several years earlier. During Dr. Lea's tenure at Bethany and in the years since, our friendship has grown, and perhaps more importantly, his ministry has prospered. I made sure I was in attendance at the revival because I wanted to see and hear him.

Dr. Lea preached from the text of James 1:1-8 (NIV):

1 James, a servant of God and of the Lord Jesus Christ,

To the twelve tribes scattered among the nations: Greetings.

2 Consider it pure joy, my brothers and sisters, whenever you face trials of many kinds,

3 because you know that the testing of your faith produces perseverance.

4 Let perseverance finish its work so that you may be mature and complete, not lacking anything.

5 If any of you lacks wisdom, you should ask God, who gives generously to all without finding fault, and it will be given to you.

6 But when you ask, you must believe and not doubt, because the one who doubts is like a wave of the sea, blown and tossed by the wind.

7 That person should not expect to receive anything from the Lord.

8 Such a person is double-minded, and unstable in all they do.

As I sat, listening intently, it occurred to me that I'd been living this text throughout my journey with cancer. By God's grace and mercy, I'd experienced true joy in the midst of my "trials of many kinds" and the "testing of my faith produced perseverance." I'd come through cancer more "mature and complete, not lacking anything."

Praise God, I was awake in the moment!

Over the years since battling cancer, people have repeatedly asked me, "What have you learned? How have you changed? How have you grown?" A relative even remarked, "You must feel like you've been given a second chance." I instantly replied, "Not really. It feels more like a promotion!"

For me, cancer was a mixed blessing. As harrowing an ordeal as it was, I learned more about me—about how I show up in times of crisis. I learned more about my loved ones and friends and how they, too, show up in times of crisis. And I learned more about God—how He shows up in times of crisis, or rather, how He's always there. Borrowing lines from the song "Day By Day" from the musical *Godspell,* I got to "see God more clearly, follow Him more nearly, and love Him more dearly." He moved me to a place where I no longer sweat the small stuff—a place where my mind is free of the clutter that can hold me back.

I'm still learning. And I'm appreciating more and more that with the gift of learning comes the responsibility of sharing the learning.

As unpredictable as life is, some things are certain. If you're born, at some point you're going to die. Good and bad things are going to happen in-between. How you approach and show up during the good and the bad, and who you show up with, makes all the difference.

When I look back over this "bad thing" (my ordeal with cancer) my words to my mother when she first visited me in the hospital after we learned about my illness resonate all the more, even for me. Concerning my diagnosis, I had declared to my mother, "It's just a part of my journey." Somehow I knew cancer would be an important chapter in my life, but not the only chapter. It might have been the last, but it wasn't going to be the defining chapter. I believe I knew because I'd actually been preparing. I believe I knew because I'd learned to trust God. I believe I knew because I was living my purpose.

Preparing for the Storm

"I have told you these things so that in Me you may have peace. You will have suffering in this world. Be courageous! I have conquered the world" (John 16:33, HCSB).

On a hot summer afternoon in 2012, more than two and a half years after my transplant and more than a year and a half after returning to work, I had lunch with a stranger. His name was Robert. I'd been a part of a marketing contest in connection with the AT&T series entitled, "Rethink Possible." The series consisted of four stories about the personal journeys and experiences of people who have done or experienced something extraordinary. Due to the handiwork of Peggy, my close friend and a marketing executive, I was featured in the series, alongside our good friend and Pulitzer Prize winner, playwright Lynn Nottage; actor and singer, Tyrese Gibson; and technology expert and television personality, Mario Armstrong. Robert, a young attorney living in Philadelphia, got something out of my segment about my journey battling leukemia, and he wanted to meet me. Based on his response to the contest, he'd won a lunch date with me.

As soon as we sat down at the restaurant table, the conversation took off. Robert was intrigued by my journey with cancer from beginning to end. He asked lots of questions about the disease and the physical toll on my body, about transplant and the science behind it, and about the psychological impact on my family and me. For most of our lunch, he asked the questions everyone else had asked me, and I answered effortlessly with words and sentences I'd strung together at least a dozen times before.

Then, to my surprise, Robert went off script and asked me a question I'd never fielded. An innocent, yet provocative, question.

Robert asked, "So, before you got cancer, did you know the Lord?"

Having professed earlier in our conversation that he was a "young Christian," what was on his mind made a lot of sense, but I was still surprised.

I was caught off guard, but I wasn't stumped. I looked at Robert and instantly replied, "Yes, I knew the Lord, and I'd been preparing for my illness."

Robert looked confused. How could I have prepared for an environmentally-caused cancer that came out of nowhere? I'd told him earlier in our conversation that I thought I had the flu. In his mind, I'm sure he was thinking, *How could she possibly have been preparing for this? And besides, who prepares to be sick?*

I began talking a mile a minute.

"My daddy used to preach about the storms of life—the events that turn our lives upside down, sometimes with little or no warning, causing devastation and despair for everyone in their paths. Daddy would say, 'Every one of us is either in a storm, coming out of a storm, or about to go through one. No one goes through life without experiencing storms.'"

I went on, "Do you remember in 2011 when the weather forecasters predicted Hurricane Irene would hit the Northeast coast with a force so great cities would have to stand still and wait it out to avert a great catastrophe? Do you remember how we all listened to the weatherman and then made preparations to get through the storm? Do you remember how we went to the grocery stores and stocked up on nonperishable items for the weekend, bought candles in case we lost electricity, brought outdoor furniture inside, took emergency money out of the ATM, boarded up windows, and helped out our elderly family members and friends? Anything we could do, we did to get ready for the storm. The meteorologists told us the storm was coming, and we did all we could to be ready and to get through it."

Taking a breath, I continued.

"Well, cancer was like that hurricane for me. It was my storm, and because of my relationship with the Lord, I was prepared for it. Had it not been for the foundation in Christ that my mother and father gave me, I may not have known how to weather my storm. Had I not understood, as the Bible teaches, that even those who profess Jesus Christ as Lord and Savior will suffer, I may have lost hope. I knew my storm was coming long before it hit. I didn't know how it would manifest, but I knew it was coming."

Blessed with a good husband and children, with loving and caring parents, a meaningful and rewarding career, and with good health, people often remarked, "Jennifer has it all." Their words made me uncomfortable. Whenever I heard such statements, I would pray that when my storm came—whatever it was—that God would help me to endure, to stay strong, and to keep smiling.

Cancer was my epic storm. I couldn't run or hide. But because I'd been preparing I was ready. Well, as ready as I could be. I'd been praying and talking with God long before my storm hit that He would strengthen me for the battle, however it presented. I didn't know the enemy, but I knew there would be one.

Lunch that day didn't turn out at all the way I anticipated it would. I walked into the restaurant believing that the purpose of lunch was for me to share my life and story with Robert, and in doing so, encourage him. Perhaps our talk did just that. However, what transpired as a result of Robert's query revealed an even greater purpose for our lunch. Robert had come to New York City carrying a message in the form of a question for me. What may have seemed a simple question was actually the key that unlocked the mystery of my earliest responses to cancer.

Why did I not fall apart upon learning I had cancer? Because I'd been preparing.

Trusting God Means Trusting the Process

"Wait for the Lord; be strong and take heart and wait for the Lord" *(Psalm 27:14, NIV).*

When I reflect on my journey, I take pride in having been able to withstand the challenges and disappointments that came with battling leukemia and pushing through the transplant on most days, but I also am humbled knowing there were several moments when "par for the course" was just too much. Some days, I dreaded going up and down the steps in the house because I felt weak and my legs were wobbly. Some days, eating was torture because I couldn't taste the food and keep it down, and my throat was sore from all of the vomiting. Going to bed at night only to have to wake up every two hours to take pills and to go to the bathroom was sometimes more exhausting than trying to stay up all night. Not being able to hug my son for fear he might be carrying germs crushed me every time he entered my bedroom.

Just about once every week, and sometimes twice, I experienced late night fevers accompanied by vomiting and diarrhea. Within hours, I'd become dehydrated. Inevitably I'd wind up in the emergency room with Shawn—or Mom and Leigh when Shawn was away on business—and then I'd be admitted for fluids and observation. Every time this happened, it hurt just knowing that Channing and Kennedy would be waking up the next morning to go to school, only to learn I wasn't there, much like they had experienced around the time when we first learned I had cancer. Sometimes it was just too much. But I kept going as best I could.

During one unplanned hospital stay in early June, I just couldn't take it anymore. For weeks, I'd been thinking ahead and looking forward to seeing Kennedy dance in Mark Morris' student company's year-end performance. Watching her dance always makes me happy because her movements are full of poise and grace, and her facial expressions suggest she is swept up in the moment, enjoying herself immensely.

I had a severe flare up of GVHD just days before the Saturday event. Weak and dehydrated, I was admitted to the hospital and was intravenously medicated with steroids to fight the disease. The doctors advised me that it was highly likely I would have to stay in the hospital over the weekend.

When I heard this news, all joy left me. I succumbed to the anger and frustration that was in me. Perhaps self-pity was always there, but I had suppressed it. I was hurting. I wanted badly to be at Kennedy's performance. Earlier that week it seemed I would be there, and then I got sick. This epic battle with its endless ups and downs was pissing me off. I was fed up with the process. I just wanted to be there for Kennedy.

As I lay in the hospital bed, frustrated and bitter, a social worker stopped by to see me. She was the social worker who interviewed me prior to transplant to assess my emotional stamina. Never had she come to see me during my transplant stay, I presume because I had not previously shown any signs of needing the support of a social worker. Clearly she'd been summoned. My frustration was showing.

The social worker sat with me for a while and asked several questions about how I was feeling. I answered all of her questions, some less truthfully than others in an attempt to convey an image of control. But judging by her questions that followed my answers, I wasn't fooling her. She was seeing through the invisible wall I was attempting to build in her very presence.

I tried to outsmart her. I answered her questions with statements that conveyed both control and vulnerability to give her enough of what I thought she needed to feel like she was doing her job well and to conclude that I was in a healthy state of mind. She saw through that too.

After about five minutes of what seemed a futile game, she asked me a game-changing question: "Who do you trust?"

I had no idea what she wanted to hear. What response could I give that would put me on top and end this annoying back and forth?

I didn't answer, and so she asked again, "Who do you trust?"

I had no clue what she was expecting to hear. So I just shrugged my shoulders and replied, "God. I trust God."

Immediately, she responded, "Well, if you trust God, then you must trust the process."

Whoa!

What she said hit home immediately. She was right. If I truly trusted God, then I had to trust that there was a reason He was allowing me to struggle. My suffering was a necessary part of the journey. Having GVHD, being hospitalized, and possibly missing Kennedy's performance were all part of the process. If I wanted to be made well, to be completely healed, then I had to go through these critical phases of transplant recovery. The more expedient path could prove deadly. If I had to miss a dance performance in order to see many more, then so be it. That's what I had to do.

Once this exchange happened, so much became clearer and more bearable. In the midst of my journey, I began seeing how God's hand was all over this "process." When I first became ill, none of us knew or suspected I had cancer. Without doubt we would have moved to get me into Memorial Sloan Kettering Cancer Center—arguably the nation's leading cancer center—as the first order of business. But God had another process. Based on an EMT decision, I wound up in St. Vincent's Hospital, a community hospital that didn't even have a blood cancer specialist, but did have praying physicians who also were expert in handling crises, and I was treated successfully.

Before Shawn and I even had the chance to seek a second opinion about my diagnosis and treatment plan, the doctor at St. Vincent's Hospital sought the advice of the leukemia specialist at New York-Presbyterian Weill Cornell Medical Center, and together they devised the best possible treatment plan for me.

As soon as I was in remission and released, the physician at St. Vincent's referred me to that same leukemia specialist, and I became her patient. She took me through two rounds of consolidation chemo and made it a priority to find me a viable transplant option.

After learning that my siblings weren't viable donors, that there wasn't already a potential donor in the national donor registry for me, and that none of the 13,000 newly registered donors added by our efforts matched me, we still didn't lose hope. We trusted God, and in turn, the process. And God provided a cord blood.

When the time came for the cord blood transplant, my doctor at New York-Presbyterian took the first step to have my case considered by a leading cord blood transplant specialist at Memorial Sloan Kettering Cancer Center. Just a few weeks later, I underwent transplant there.

We'd done nothing but trust the process for battling leukemia from induction and consolidation treatment pre-transplant, to transplant, and then post-transplant, just as the doctors had laid it out—taking the necessary steps and following specific guidelines.

Fighting for my life while raising two young children was hard enough. Doing so while trying to maintain some normalcy in their lives, especially during holidays when sentimentality is at its peak, would have seemed impossible. But somehow it all worked out. More than nine months of touch and go, and we never missed celebrating a holiday together as a family.

After being diagnosed on Kennedy's birthday, of all days, and then hospitalized for more than five weeks in the earliest days of my illness, I was released the day before Halloween. I was unexpectedly hospitalized just days before Thanksgiving, but released in time to cook corn pudding and candied yams, Kennedy and Channing's holiday favorites, for that special day. Shawn and I celebrated our wedding anniversary by having breakfast and lunch together and going Christmas shopping, as we had routinely done on our special day. My second round of in-patient consolidation was scheduled two days following Channing's birthday party and ended in time for me to celebrate his actual birthday and Christmas at home with all of my siblings, their families, and my immediate family. I got to bring in the New Year with Shawn, the kids, Mom, and Elsa before becoming seriously ill with an infection in my lungs that put me in the ICU three days later. We baked a birthday cake for Martin Luther King, Jr. together, just as we had done each year since Kennedy was four. On Valentine's Day we went to the Berkshires and the kids and Shawn skied like we'd done many times before. I went into the hospital for my transplant on Ash Wednesday, and came home on Good Friday. We had our annual Easter egg hunt and dinner on Easter Sunday, even if it was rushed because I had to go to back into the hospital. And because the doctors were willing to bend the rules just once to permit Channing, who was under twelve, to visit the transplant floor, Mom, the kids, Shawn, and I celebrated Mother's Day in the hospital when I was being treated for GVHD.

During my journey, I got to physically, mentally, and spiritually see how God was moving, how He was in control of the process. I didn't have to fret or fear. If recovery was slow, there was a reason. If I experienced a setback, it was part of the process.

All of my life God had been working it out. All of my life He'd been taking charge of the process and preparing me for my journey with cancer. All the good things and all the bad things that had happened in my life were preparation for this moment. The new friends, the lost friends, the dream jobs, the rejections, the poor decisions, the forgiveness and redemption—all of those experiences had made me stronger and increased my faith and trust in Him. All of those times God had watched over me, protected me when I did foolish things—things that could have gotten me seriously hurt or killed—they all were part of the preparation and the process.

My family was part of God's process. My husband of eighteen years, always so strong and never showing much emotion. I used to complain that he didn't emote enough. What did I know? God knew. He knew that when I was walking through the valley of the shadow of death I was going to need someone who wasn't going to fall apart, a man of faith who wasn't going to get lost in the direness of the situation but rather press on. Having my mother at my side caring for me like I was her newborn. My siblings, sister-friends, and many other friends all working on my behalf. All were part of the process. Even my deceased father. His good works lived on. Ministers were calling their church members together to pray and take action because Bill Jones' daughter was in trouble.

Everywhere I looked, I saw more than ample evidence that it was okay to let go and trust the process.

⌒

All of these occurrences might be considered by some to be mere coincidences. I vehemently disagree. However, if one is not otherwise convinced, the events that bookend the earliest days of my career and my transplant provide the most awesome affirmation.

Over twenty years ago, I went to law school, planning to become a corporate lawyer. Then one day while amid my studies, I felt myself being called by God to work as a child advocate and lawyer, to help save and improve the lives of vulnerable children. And from that day right up until the days before I learned I had leukemia—a total of seventeen years—I'd been about the business of trying to fulfill my purpose: helping to save children's lives.

Well, after learning that my siblings weren't matches for me for transplant, that there were more than eight million potential bone marrow donors in the registry but none were a viable match for me, and that 13,000 people were added to the registry as a result of our drives but none matched me, hope easily could have faded and despair taken over. We were running out of time. I couldn't undergo much more chemotherapy without it potentially having lesser effectiveness and a greater toll on my body.

But just when hopelessness could have set in and perhaps was beginning to set in for some, just when I needed someone to help save me, God sent the children—the umbilical cord blood of two little African American baby boys. Seventeen years earlier, I'd answered God's calling to help protect and save his most vulnerable children, and then, when I need someone to help save me, God sent the children.

Trust God and trust the process, and in time, His perfect plan will be made clear.

Living Your Purpose

"And we know that in all things God works for the good of those who love him, who have been called according to his purpose" (Romans 8:28, NIV).

I believe that God gives life to help fulfill His purposes, and that when we each have fulfilled His purpose for our lives, He calls us home.

Perhaps this is why, after waking up from my medically induced coma and learning of the outpouring of love and support from friends, family, colleagues, and even strangers, I declared to my sister, "This isn't about me. This is bigger than me." Because of my faith, I believed there was purpose in my suffering. Why else would God allow me to fall deathly ill? Why else would my siblings not be compatible bone marrow donors? For what other reason would there be a bone marrow registry with more than eight million registered donors, but no match for me?

My daddy once said to my mom, "There is a hell, and for some it's here on earth." Well, if battling leukemia isn't hell on earth, it's as close as I hope to ever come. There had to be a reason I was experiencing a living hell.

Before being stricken with leukemia, I knew little about the disease and the possibility of a cure with transplanted bone marrow. I knew nothing about the ease of registering and becoming a donor. It turned out that many, many others didn't know either. But when I became ill, that changed for me and thousands more. When the call went out that I needed someone to donate bone marrow to help me live, people across this nation paid attention and took action. Family and friends, colleagues and strangers, churches, sororities and fraternities, the National Action Network, the Progressive National Baptist Convention, Jack and Jill of America, my children's schools, the Black Bar Associations, colleges and universities, and New York agencies all worked feverishly to find an unrelated bone marrow donor for me and for others in need of a transplant. In just thirteen weeks, over 13,000 people registered to be a donor.

As I lay ill, I was blessed to see how God had shaped and molded me, and how He was taking the life He'd given me and was using my predicament to reach others and strengthen them and me. I experienced great joy and peace in knowing that my experience and search for a donor might help both me and so many others in need. My life had meaning. My suffering had purpose.

More than a year after transplant, while driving to work one day, I was playing one of my father's sermons in the car. As Dad preached, I listened intently. As he hit the apex of his message, he exclaimed, "Don't you know He didn't save you for your sake? He saved you for the kingdom's sake."

Upon hearing those words, I was overcome with pure joy. The tears began flowing and my heart began racing. Just as there had been purpose in my suffering, there also was purpose in my living. I am only here, still living today, because God has more for me to do.

I urge you to seek God's purpose for your life, and then strive to live your purpose as fully as you can. Your life and your purpose are bigger, much bigger, than you could ever dream.

My message to you:

Pray for clarity, embrace your reality, and live your purpose!

Perhaps the greatest harm we can do to ourselves is to not own our problems, our faults, and our weaknesses. Ignoring our bills, pretending we aren't sick, and minimizing the pain we feel in our relationships are all acts of willful denial. These and other acts of denial may allow us to escape from our burdens for fleeting moments, but they don't help us overcome them.

Pray for clarity in every aspect of your life so that you may see things as they truly are. Then, deal upfront. Confront your fear and wrestle with it, and make a conscious decision to do something about your situation. Pray, have faith, and then move to fulfill your purpose. That's what God intends for your life. That's what He has empowered you to do. That's why you're still here.

Because of Christ I Have a Choice

I choose to be happy!

I choose to be loved!

I choose to give love!

I choose to live with joy!

Me - Six Weeks Following Diagnosis and First Round of Chemotherapy

Top: My Mother and Me - Thanksgiving 2009
Bottom: Channing's 8th Birthday Party - 2009

Top: Shawn, Kennedy, Me, and Channing - Christmas 2009
Bottom Left : Kennedy and Me - Christmas 2009
Bottom Right : Channing and Me - Christmas 2009

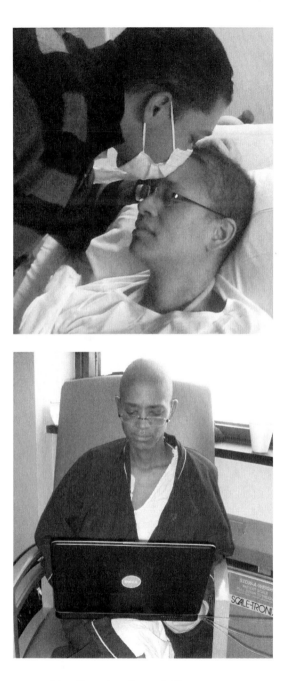

Top: Transplant Day with Shawn - 2010
Bottom: Hospital during Transplant - 2010

Top: Kennedy, Shawn, Me, and Channing - Easter 2010
Bottom: Kennedy and Me - Easter 2010

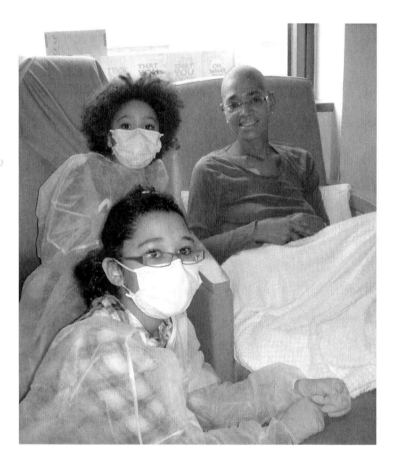

Hospital Visit on Mother's Day with Channing and Kennedy - 2010

Acknowledgements

This book is dedicated to the unsung heroes:

- the physician's assistant who surprised me with sexy "Scarlet Red" nail polish after seeing my nails had turned yellow, gray, and black from round after round of chemotherapy

- the administrative aide who, as she passed by me in the radiology waiting room, noticed that I was bald and not wearing a wig, and exclaimed, "You're beautiful!"

- the social worker who came to me during a hospital stay to provide me with an ear for listening, only to leave shortly thereafter, telling me that I inspired her

- the nurse who listened quietly to my fears about possibly having an anaphylactic reaction to a CT scan with iodine contrast—which I needed for treatment—all the while never letting on that she, herself, is allergic and also terrified

- the radiology technician who positioned my breast with one hand and gently stroked my back with the other

- the nurse who said to me, "You were chosen. How special! Like Job, chosen because God believed in you!"

- the nurses, especially Erica, who fought for me when I felt like I had no more fight left in me

- the staff and volunteers at Be The Match and Icla da Silva Foundation who had boots on the ground whenever and wherever a bone marrow drive was scheduled

- my husband, Shawn, who, during my illness, steered the ship twenty-four hours a day and never fell asleep at the wheel

- my children, Kennedy and Channing, who exemplified courage even when it would have been more than okay to buckle at the knees

- my mother, Natalie, who would have taken the hit for me if only she could

- my siblings, Billy, Elsa, and Lesley; and my cousins LaMarr, Leigh, and Robin, who journeyed with me every step of the way

- my nieces and nephews who led and assisted with drives, determined to find a match for me

- my sister-friends Anne, Andrea, Ayo, Bernie, Jamie, Kim, Melissa, Myrla, Peggy, Saadia and Theresa, and Dara, Jennifer, Shelia, Debbie, Camille, and Michelle, who went well beyond the duties attendant to friendship

- my colleagues, especially Linda, Gail, Dennis, Kathryn, Juanita, and Raysa, who transitioned immediately to friends and constant supports upon receiving word of my illness

- my children's school community, my Jack and Jill community, and our many friends who ensured Shawn and the kids never had the additional worry of what to eat

- and my church and faith community who prayed for me without ceasing

Biography

A fourth-generation leader of faith and social justice, Jennifer Jones Austin, Esq. fights for equity. As CEO of FPWA, she leads poverty fighting, policy, and advocacy efforts to strengthen and empower the disenfranchised and marginalized communities. Jennifer brings to her work a profound understanding of the link between poverty and social policy in American life, and the roles religion and faith play in addressing economic injustice.

She is a sought-after speaker who appears regularly on television and radio, and at community events and professional convenings. Jennifer guest hosts the nationally syndicated radio program, "Keep'n It Real with Rev Al Sharpton," and the cable program, *Brooklyn Savvy*. She was born and raised in New York City, and resides in Brooklyn with her husband and two almost grown children. Jennifer Jones Austin has served on numerous boards, including the National Marrow Donor Program, the Icla da Silva Foundation, and the New York Blood Center, all of which were instrumental in her search for a bone marrow donor.